PATRICIA MARNE'S
MANUAL OF
GRAPHOLOGY

PATRICIA MARNE'S MANUAL OF GRAPHOLOGY

Compiled and updated by Peter West

quantum

LONDON • NEW YORK • TORONTO • SYDNEY

quantum

An imprint of W. Foulsham & Co. Ltd
The Publishing House, Bennetts Close,
Cippenham, Slough, Berks, SL1 5AP, England

ISBN 0-572-02463-0

This book includes new text and artwork as well as
text material, examples and signatures from three
previously published works by Patricia Marne:

The Concise Graphology Notebook

Sexual Secrets in Handwriting

The Secrets in Their Signature

It has not been possible to trace all those whose
handwriting or signatures have been used in this
book. Where examples have been used to illustrate
or emphasise certain points, it has been solely for that
purpose. No personal criticism of individuals is intended.

Printed in Great Britain by St. Edmundsbury Press, Bury St. Edmunds, Suffolk.

CONTENTS

INTRODUCTION

W hen we look back through history, it is abundantly clear that formal language – writing – followed naturally and inevitably from the evolution of human speech. This development in communication itself continued to evolve and became one of the ancestors of modern printing systems, which eventually led to the complex and ever-broadening world of computers.

At first, people communicated through sound and gesture. The latter may well have changed remarkably little over thousands of years! Even today, gesture is still employed as an effective means of communication, especially between people who speak different languages, and in some instances can be more expressive than any words or writing. Speech, on the other hand, gradually changed and developed so that specific sounds came to represent particular objects, each isolated group or tribe having its own unique language.

At the same time, written communication began to develop, perhaps beginning as simple pictures painted on the walls of caves over 20,000 years ago. Startling images of hunting scenes and beautiful depictions of the sun, moon and stars still communicate to us today from all those centuries ago.

As people began to move beyond the confines of their own groups, communication and language needed to become more sophisticated. Gesture remained of particular importance, of course, but the more interaction there was between peoples, the more they needed a reliable system of expression, through both the spoken and the written word.

Seals

Once people began to establish trading contacts with other groups, some kinds of markings were needed to define ownership of goods. The first method by which this was achieved was by using labels of clay, some in colour and others bearing representative symbols.

It was not long before these labels began to bear seals, impressed marks which represented the name of the owner, and soon just the seal alone became not only a method of identifying the owner of the goods but also, by implication, a symbol of the individual trader. A simple seal would communicate not just a name but also a reputation, and traders were recognised through their personal seal for their fairness and honesty – or otherwise. Such seals are still used today in the form of company logos, perhaps the most readily recognised symbol of major business organisations all over the world. If you consider for a moment the Olympic rings, you will instantly realise that it takes only a split second for that symbol to communicate to you sporting achievement, international co-operation, patriotism, fairness – and perhaps quite a few other concepts as well. The same is true – although perhaps the connotations are different! – of the McDonald's 'M', the Coca-Cola symbol or the Red Cross.

Although seals were not themselves the precursors of handwriting, they do represent one of the origins of written communication and, with the concept of these seals in mind, it is easy to see how a person's style of written communication – their writing – has since become inextricably associated with character and personality.

The alphabet and writing systems

Early writing actually began with hieroglyphic forms: pictures which represented the object in question. While this clearly works well for simple nouns such as bison, arrow or man, confusion is introduced when you want to communicate other concepts such as tall, quiet, love or close. Gradually, therefore, written language became idiomatic, leading eventually to the development of the alphabet.

The first known forms of alphabet and writing were developed by the peoples of the Sumerian civilisation. Sumer, which was situated roughly in the area of modern Iraq, is generally regarded as the cradle of modern civilisation. Although it is the source of the first attempts at creating an alphabet, so many changes, additions and deletions have been made over the centuries that we would hardly recognise these original attempts as the forerunner of our own 26-letter English language alphabet – let alone the other alphabets now in use around the world.

Besides the actual words used, handwriting must conform to specific rules in order to be properly understood. In modern Western cultures, we normally begin on the left-hand side of the paper and write in a straight line across the page. When we reach the right-hand side of the paper, we leave a space and begin again below the first line and repeat the process, continuing in this way until our narrative is finished.

In earlier times, handwriting was created in various styles, one of which alternated the direction of the script from line to line. This was called *boustrophedon* writing, or 'ox-turning'. It was of Greek origin and was based on the way an ox was made to plough a furrow across a field one way, then turn and plough a parallel furrow in the other direction. This system had largely died out by around the fifth century BC.

Other writing systems have survived and so in other modern cultures, the direction of writing may be from right to left or up and down the page.

Handwriting as a means of recognition

As with any innovation, once the concept of communication through the written word was established, it quickly began to develop and flourish, eventually becoming one of the major means of communication between people. While the technological revolution which occurred over the latter part of the twentieth century has resulted in a shift of balance away from the handwritten word, we still recognise the importance of handwriting and its association with character and personality.

A person's handwriting is as much a part of their character as the way they look, speak or walk, and is just as useful a method of recognition. When a letter drops on to our doormat, the first thing we do is to look at the writing on the envelope to see if we can recognise the sender. We can instantly sort out the circulars, followed by the computer-printed business letters, but receiving a handwritten letter makes it something more special and personal. Most people will look at the handwritten envelope first and instantly recognise the writing style of a close friend. Even if the script is unknown to us, we still look at it and try to work out who sent it, when the most obvious thing to do would be to open it!

We develop our handwriting throughout childhood, beginning on the foundation of the basic alphabet and handwriting style which we have learnt in school. As our individual abilities emerge and become established, so does our handwriting. Gradually, we speed up, we add little bits here, eliminate little things there, and personalise the common style, so that in a very short time the handwriting styles of a group of children who have all learned to write together will begin to diverge and become reflections of their own characters and personalities. Of course, this all takes time. As we progress, each of us eventually begins to use a unique style that friends come to associate with us and our personality.

As we become familiar with the handwriting of our friends, we also associate their style with certain aspects of their personalities. We may also notice that people with similar personalities have similarities in their style of handwriting: think about the broad, sweeping signature of the extrovert or the tiny, precise writing of the well-organised scientist. This rather informal introduction to handwriting analysis is something we all do instinctively. We may not always realise the value it could have if we only carried it out in a more disciplined way.

A definition of graphology

Graphology is the study and analysis of handwriting for the purpose of interpreting personality and character. Normally, the assessment will not confirm the sex or age of the writer, although handwriting may show indications of age if the writer is elderly. It can, however, indicate all kinds of personality traits, from emotional maturity and creative ability to physical attributes and mental potential. Graphology is only one of many tools helpful in determining character and personality, but is nonetheless a helpful tool which can be used along with other methods of assessment.

There are plenty of ways in which this can be useful: assessing vocational talents, assisting in personnel selection or advising on emotional compatibility, for example.

For a young person trying to select a career, a graphological assessment made at the right time can help to shape their career and future path by identifying latent talents and appropriate directions for them to consider. In a case where a child shows an aptitude for an occupation but their parents want to guide them into another path – perhaps in the search for higher status or financial rewards, or even to fulfil an ambition of the parents themselves – graphology can help to establish the best direction to take.

Of course, some young people have the knack of doing precisely the opposite of what is expected of them, especially by their parents, and no amount of assessment can stop that from happening in some cases!

Having made a career selection, an unfortunately large number of people decide that they have made a bad choice and would be better to try something else. This is not an easy decision to take, and far too many people stay with their current occupation even though experience has shown that they are totally unsuited to it. Again, graphology can usually help to point the way and help them to find something far more fulfilling.

From the business executive's point of view, identifying the right person for a job in their company can be a daunting task. The support of a graphology assessment of the candidates can be immensely useful in making the right decisions.

Since handwriting also displays our personal characteristics, it is not unusual for people to use a handwriting assessment as a means of finding out more about a potential partner, whether in a business or personal sense.

The origins of graphology
Strictly speaking, graphology is quite a modern practice.

It is true that centuries ago, it was accepted up to a point that an individual could be identified through their handwriting style, although looking back at the source of this information shows that we must be careful not to make too many assumptions. In his book *De Vita Caesarum, (The Lives of the Caesars)*, in AD 120, Suetonius Tranquillus complained of the handwriting of Octavius Augustus because the writer seemed unable to plan and space his writing properly. He was, in fact, noticing aspects which demonstrated certain characteristics in Octavius' handwriting, but he was not drawing those conclusions from his comments. He was criticising the writing simply because it was difficult to read. Of course, it is perfectly feasible that the work was not written by Octavius at all but by a scribe, in which case he was very much to blame, since his job was to write manuscripts clearly! This example does serve to illustrate, however, that nearly 2,000 years ago, people were very much aware of the importance of handwriting and written presentation.

Although writing and writing styles were known and discussed in China as early as the fourth century AD, it was not until 1622 that a European work of any real note appeared on the subject. Camillo Baldi, of the University of Bologna, in Italy, is credited with being one of the founding fathers of modern handwriting analysis. His small work claimed that handwriting was very much a personal matter and could reflect the character to some extent. This book was followed in 1792 by another, this time the work of Professor Grohmann of Wittenberg, in Germany, who made similar observations.

It is well known that the British artist Thomas Gainsborough was fascinated by the idea of character analysis through handwriting, for he kept letters written by his model of the moment on his easel while he painted their portrait. The writer Sir Walter Scott makes considerable reference to graphology in his 1827 book, *Chronicles of the Canongate*, in which he discusses the relative merits of handwriting analysis.

Perhaps the most important step forward in the history of handwriting analysis must lie with a Frenchman, the Abbé Michon, who in 1871 introduced the term 'graphology'. He was the first to research a scientific basis for the study and to lay the basic ground rules – a high percentage of which are still observed today. After this, many people share the credit for advancing interest in graphology – far too many to go into detail here. Since the turn of the twentieth century, however, there have been many advances in the study.

Art or science?

Graphology is neither an art nor a science – it is both. The graphologist must employ a scientific approach in order to recognise and evaluate all the basic factors in the writing under review. The art lies in bringing together all the traits to synthesise what is found into a descriptive portrait. Clearly this is affected by the individual analyst's personal experience of life and of graphology. Many graphologists use their natural intuition when they are working on a character analysis, and it is also helpful to have some knowledge of and interest in psychology. Unless you possess the most basic grounding about what makes people tick, you will not be able to do justice to them, or indeed to yourself.

Graphology is a true art-science and for it to serve you, and for you to serve it, you must be able to blend the technicalities with the artistry – in all its forms. The more you practise, the more insight you gain into the behaviour patterns of others and, as an additional benefit, the more it will help you to understand yourself.

Basic rules of interpretation

Handwriting analysis has two marvellous advantages over all the other personality assessment systems. A properly analysed script will produce a most accurate picture of its author at the time it was written; and there are very few areas in which a handwriting analyst may not be employed. The following basic principles will act as a base for your study of the detailed elements of the craft.

Perhaps the most important fundamental of graphological analysis is that the analyst must remember that handwriting reflects the mood and thinking of the writer at the time of writing. There are a few, very few, exceptions and these will all be dealt with in full later in this book. Within the same sample of handwriting, there may therefore be quite considerable variations, which reflect the changing mood and disposition of the writer at the time the script was executed.

When you write a note asking a family member or friend to do something for you, you physically write in exactly the same way as you would to prepare an application for an important promotion. What's more, your character does not change between writing one and writing the other. Much more time and care would be put into making a job application compared with a brief note, however, and this will show clearly in the writing specimens, as will the underlying style of the handwriting and your own underlying personality.

Whatever the subject matter, most of us are fairly self-conscious at the start of any letter, note or other missive, but interest in keeping our writing neat and tidy tends to fade as we proceed. As a rule, therefore, most handwriting examples are likely to be more naturally executed at the end than at the beginning. So one of the first thing many experts do is to look at the end first. It is there that our most natural handwriting is found and this will therefore be most revealing to the graphologist.

The health of the writer, their mood and the speed with which the handwriting appears to have been executed all have their bearing on the final analysis. Thus, you must always observe and evaluate the whole script – never just a part of it.

Never hesitate to pick up a pen or pencil to trace a letter, word or even a whole line here and there to see for yourself how the writer originally produced it. This is always helpful in your assessment because although handwriting is largely a logical process – we have all learned in the first place to form our letters in roughly the same way – it is often unconsciously executed. This will be explained more fully as we work through the book.

The way the main body of the text is set out on the page yields information on the emotional, mental and physical outlook of the writer – at the time of writing, remember. It reflects the real or 'inner' person.

The signature will show the way in which the writer would like to be seen by others – their 'outer' image. This is why many people have two quite different signatures. They use one for formal or business life and keep the other for their more personal, private and intimate matters. This is one very good reason why it is wiser not to analyse a signature on its own. Two, three or even four examples would better or, at the very least, some other text with which you may compare the writer's two natures. With only one example, the graphologist might still be able to detect quite a lot about the writer, but it is not really a practical exercise as the analysis would be very incomplete.

Always retain handwritten envelopes for there is an element of control in the way envelopes are addressed. It is always worthwhile making an assessment and comparison of the handwriting of a letter with that on the accompanying envelope.

A much neglected area of analysis is the way numbers are written and also how they are used to create the date. Quite often this will show the age of the writer or when and where they were educated. Note also, in your analysis, how figures are used in sums of money and the symbol of the money system employed – '£' for the pounds sterling, '$' for dollars and so on.

The colour of ink normally used by the writer also says much about their inner emotional character and personality, although it is important to make sure that they regularly use the same colour and you are not basing your conclusions on a note dashed off in the heat of the moment with whatever was to hand.

The same principle applies to the colour of the paper. Most people use white paper, or shades varying from pure white to cream. However, some people like to use plain paper of another colour, or perhaps paper of differing shades of the same colour, or even multi-coloured paper. As long as this is a regular feature, take it all into account in your analysis, but do make sure that you do not let your own preferences interfere with your objectivity. A letter with handwriting in a pale mauve ink on a bright green and orange paper might create a picture in your mind that could detract from a later logical analysis!

How to approach a graphology assessment

Whenever you are analysing a piece of handwriting, it is essential to consider all the elements as a whole, and not rely too much on one piece of evidence. Work through all the different aspects of your assessment, making notes as you go along, and gradually build up a picture of the subject which takes every clue and signal into account. Don't be too hasty to make a judgement, as you may find that different aspects of the handwriting will strike a balance as you proceed with your examination, and different aspects may strengthen or soften a characteristic. Remember that everyone is unique and complex and you must be wary, especially while you are gaining experience, of being too dogmatic in your character analysis.

Copy and use the forms at the back of this book to make sure you do not forget any aspects of your analysis. Make sure you have read the whole book before you start, then work through the topics in each chapter, writing down details of the the handwriting and initial assessments as you go. Only when you have come to the end should you try and piece together the whole picture and create a character analysis which is as accurate as possible.

Test your own handwriting

Finally, it has become fashionable in many books to recommend that new readers should stop at the end of an introduction and pause for a moment before reading any further. This is useful for a student of graphology as it provides the ideal moment to write a short note – either to someone you know well or even to yourself – to be read at a later date.

It should be on plain, unlined white A4 or standard-sized paper. You should use a fountain pen or a ball-point, not a pencil or a fibre-tip. It does not matter too much what you write as long as it is in your usual style. About 100 words or so will suffice and you should sign it with your usual signature – or signatures if you have more than one for professional and personal use. Date the sample and put it away in an envelope, which should be properly addressed either to the friend or to yourself at your own home address. Keep it safe until you have read this book.

Afterwards, you will be free to make as impartial a judgement as possible of your own handwriting ...

Chapter 1

FORM LEVEL

The form level of a piece of writing is the primary impression a graphologist has of the overall handwriting before he or she begins to study individual letters and strokes. When the overall look of the handwriting has been appraised, the graphologist can move on to evaluate each single trait that appears in the sample. The form level reveals the writer's whole personality and shows their level of intelligence and maturity.

Although it is one of the first things the graphologist considers, it is not easy to make an accurate assessment of form level and it takes a lot of experience. The complexities of human nature are many and varied, and nowhere is this more clearly illustrated than in handwriting. The graphologist must therefore use a combination of experience and intuition in order to make an assessment, because any piece of handwriting will inevitably reveal contradictory traits. This underlines the importance of a knowledge of psychology in the study of graphology, as well as an understanding of the specifics of the subject.

Many eminent psychologists and psychiatrists, including Carl Jung and Sigmund Freud, showed a strong interest in graphology and even studied the subject, with positive findings. They found that what is now called the 'expressive movement' in handwriting is as revealing as a person's physical movements and gestures because both are performed unconsciously. Not everyone realises that such expressive movements – be it in gesture or handwriting – can be interpreted as indicators of character, but they provide a wealth of information to the trained eye.

We do not fully understand why handwriting should reveal character and personality in this way, although it is clear that in the same way that instructions are sent from the brain to parts of the body to control gesture and movement, specific instructions from the brain also dictate the movements of the hand. Perhaps 'brainwriting' could be another name for handwriting. When these movements are unconscious, as is the case with instinctive gesture and handwriting, then the person is expressing what they are really like and not how they want to be perceived.

Again, it is because these expressive movements are unconscious that they provide such an accurate guide to interpreting the writer's character. No matter how hard anyone tries to disguise their handwriting, individual traits will be detected by the trained eye of the graphologist. You may think that there will be differences, depending on whether you write a note in a hurry or take your time writing a special letter. However, although the slowly written letter may be neater to look at or easier to read, both examples will have the same basic characteristics.

The form level of any handwriting will depend on the way a writer has developed their style since they first learned to write at school. It is therefore essential to know where the subject received their basic education. Different countries have their own methods, style and emphasis in teaching children to write. Requirements in American schools are quite different from those in the UK, and these, in turn, are not the same as those in Spain, Germany or Denmark. If the graphologist is working in one country, they will have experience of that country's most basic handwriting considerations. If they look at samples from people who have been educated in a different country, they must familiarise themselves with the appropriate writing style.

The next element to consider when looking at a sample is the assessment of the apparent intelligence of the writer. The graphologist can assess the speed or slowness of the script, together with the development of individuality, or how far the writer has created their own unique style from the original they were taught when they first attended school. The first example on page 19 is called print script and was introduced into the English education system in the 1930s. Children were taught to print their letters and only later moved on to learn 'joined-up' writing.

ABCDEFGHIJKLM
NOPQRSTUVWXYZ
abcdefghijklm
nopqrstuvwxyz

More recently, the cursive style of the following example has been adopted so that children move naturally from a cursive print to a flowing handwriting without a break. Styles taught in schools vary, and in some cases both a print and cursive style may be used.

ABCDEFGHIJKLM
NOPQRSTUVWXYZ
abcdefghijklm
nopqrstuvwxyz

If an adult were to write exactly in either of these two basic styles without the expected usual personal embellishments, your first assumption might reasonably be that they are a fairly boring character: hesitant, unoriginal, with little flair, one who toes the line and is a follower rather than a leader. They may be relatively intelligent but will lack perception and initiative. They are not likely to be dishonest, just rather ordinary and mundane.

The following example has been written with some speed and it bears little or no relation to the first alphabet. This illustrates what is called a high form level. Here, it is obvious the writer has developed a quick, perceptive mind and is original in their overall approach. Speed indicates spontaneity. From this we can deduce a certain amount of style and a potential for leadership.

> *I have previously requested but unfortunately it wa: I would appreciate anoth will look after it more car*

High form level

In addition we also have to judge how much pressure is applied, assess the spacing and look for naturalness in the script. In the following example of original form level, the pressure is firm and the writing looks natural and unaffected. The spacing is slightly uneven but overall the style is fairly original. Remember, by originality you must judge by how much the writer deviates from the basic school alphabet construction. The less variation there is, the less adventurous the writer will be. They will tend to stick to the rules and may well prefer others to lead, for they do not like to make mistakes or be seen to do so. Thus, the more the writer personalises their script, the more individual their nature.

> *ng history, I who I wish t l of, so a bit of contrivan rovide enough contact whilst out what a damn good c*

Original form level

When assessing the spacing, you should look at the arrangement of the whole letter on the page. This must include margins, word and line spacing and the spacing of letters within words. Spacing should look natural, not forced or irregular. Spacing between lines and words reveals whether the state of mind of the writer is erratic or orderly, whether or not they have clear or muddled thinking. A well-spaced letter with lines and words at an equal distance is an indication of mature thinking with the ability to assimilate emotional experiences and maintain integrity. It also shows good organisational ability and well-developed planning capacity. We will deal with spacing in more detail later.

So by looking at the form level of the writing, we begin to build up a picture of the writer's personality.

Chapter 2

RHYTHM

The rhythm of handwriting delivers an overall impression of the mental, physical and spiritual forces of the writer. It expresses the writer's vitality and character and shows the individual impulses which must be taken into consideration along with other traits when evaluating personality. Rhythmic traits in handwriting indicate the intensity and scope of the functional energies – self-control, will-power, mental stability – in relation to the natural impulses. It shows how that balance, or imbalance, is achieved and maintained in the person's character, a very important feature when looking at the overall personality of an individual, how they work and what they are capable of achieving.

Harmonious, even handwriting denotes that the biological impulses of the writer are intact; there is little in the way of physical or mental disturbance to upset their equilibrium. Unrhythmic handwriting, on the other hand, shows the writer suffers from inner conflicts, many of which could have remained unresolved from their formative years into adulthood.

To establish whether handwriting is rhythmic or unrhythmic, look at the connecting strokes, the speed, the spacing and formation of letters and the slant of the writing. The degree to which these attributes are apparent in the writing will indicate the level of balance in the person's character.

Rhythmic traits

Rhythmic writing indicates personal harmony, an even distribution of the emotions and impulses, and an economical use of energies.

This is particularly the case when the script tends to remain rhythmic throughout the sample.

When handwriting flows evenly and the spacing, pressure and size are well balanced, with the letters all of a reasonable height and the up and down strokes of approximately the same size, it indicates strong will-power and a high degree of self-control. The psychological impulses that influence this writer mean that the intellect exerts a stronger force than the emotions, and that makes for regularity and control.

The right-slanted, rhythmic handwriting below, with its well-balanced letter formation, shows a consistent mind and good mental control.

Where there is over-control, however, the handwriting becomes rigid and without spontaneity (see below). This is a sign of potential obsessional behaviour and an almost compulsive inhibition, preventing the writer from developing a more relaxed personality. The natural instincts are suppressed, and monotonous or compulsive behaviour can be the result. This very inflexible style shows a person who exerts too much self-discipline, resulting in inhibition. The writer maintains such a tight control of their emotions at all times that this acts to the detriment of any natural spontaneity.

Unrhythmic traits

When there are large gaps between letters and words, or varying slants within a script showing changes of direction, these factors indicate that there is irregular movement of the hand during writing, implying that the writer has not established a consistent balance between their emotions and their mental self-discipline.

Such writing often reveals a strong creative or artistic ability and a person who leads an active emotional life. However, it can also indicate fluctuating levels of self-assurance and a tendency to moodiness and abrupt changes of temper. This person's mind is active with emotional intensity, and they may be impulsive especially under pressure. In extreme cases, there may be a tendency to unreliability or even instability of the sympathetic nervous system.

Such writers tend to be restless, often suffering from anxiety (real or imagined) in their make-up. Because they lack will-power, they are torn between their natural impulses and maintaining a tighter control of their mind and emotions. This can lead to poor control and a lack of self-restraint.

There is an erratic slant to the example of script below, indicating the writer's inability to remain consistent in thought and action. The varying slant, size and pressure all reveal a restless, mercurial mind.

> be defined as a the study and
> and writing to interpret characte
> lity. The graphologist cannot
> nature and does not need extra-
> ption or an over-developed
> analyse a sample of script,
> and experience he or she

Occasionally, young people unconsciously adopt an irregular script as it seems to express their emerging personality more fully and indicates that they do not respect the demand to conform.

Chapter 3

RELEASE AND RESTRAINT

The released or restrained factor in handwriting furnishes yet more clues to the writer's personality. When a pen is held rigidly in the hand, the writing muscles are tense and this restricts the movement of the pen, causing the script to be formed in a restrained manner. The writing often appears as a monotonous row of conforming letters, taut and controlled.

When handwriting flows freely and smoothly, it shows fluency and vitality because of the freedom of that movement. Most people's handwriting falls between these two extremes; neither too rigid nor too loose, having characteristics of both but not carried to either extreme.

If handwriting is controlled and rigid, it indicates that the emotional life of the writer may suffer because they find it difficult to relax. They can often seem to be uptight or anxious. They may, perhaps, conform a little too much and do what other people expect them to do rather what they might like to do in any given set of circumstances.

People with a restrained style of handwriting can have difficulty in expressing their emotions spontaneously and tend to allow the head to rule the heart all the time. This is liable to make them view any impulsive gestures of affection as 'soft'. Even though they want to let their loved ones know how much they care, they stifle their feelings. A much more tolerant and relaxed attitude would release the pent-up tension thus created by the writer.

Such rigid and controlled script as in the following sample shows that the writer is highly independent but emotionally repressed, unable to let their feelings out. This writer tries to keep both their emotions and thoughts under very strong control and, as a consequence, misses out on the aspects of life which demand a degree of spontaneity.

Dont let the work pile up
or it only creates quite a

The left-slanted but narrow script below belongs to a far more relaxed person, but there are still some tightly controlled feelings which prevent the writer from showing a lot of warmth or affection. There are, however, some rounded strokes which indicate a warmth of character. Good judgement is also shown by the unlooped descenders.

Please find enclosed Several
Photo - copies of my hands
which I hope will be Sufficient
for you to work from . I'am

This right-facing slant flows easily without any restrictions. It has a rhythmic quality about it which is basically a symbol of the writer's need to communicate and find companionship – a reaching out to the world and to other people. Writers with this kind of style have a far more tolerant and spontaneous nature than the person who writes in a rigid script, and they can act impulsively or demonstrate warmth without embarrassment. While they are more relaxed and outgoing, there is still a need for affection.

revealed in handwriting
...e along here to find
...y be discovered in mind

Below is another sample of rounded and right-slanting handwriting that illustrates a feeling nature, warm and affectionate with a sensitive and perceptive streak. The writer is capable of many friendships and expresses emotions freely – they are likely to be far happier in love than the restrained type.

better to have loved

to have loved at all.

Although this next handwriting is rounded and basically non-aggressive, the writer's hand does not flow as easily as in the previous example. This writer holds on to their emotions, they are kind and sensitive with an impressionable nature. The left-sloping underlengths of the g and the y suggest that they sometimes hide their true thoughts and feelings through a streak of cautiousness.

and I am looking
to that very much!

When handwriting slants forward to the right and slopes upward, it shows a good social attitude, a need for communication, a high level of intelligence and the ability to think rapidly.

This right-slanted script with slightly angular strokes denotes an energetic person who is impatient and impulsive. Sociable, but often irritable, they drive themselves too hard. Their emotional life probably suffers because of a lack of thoughtfulness and a rather careless attitude towards others.

The most beautiful
place in the world is

Chapter 4

LEFT HAND, RIGHT HAND

Throughout history, in just about any sphere of activity you care to investigate, there has always been a marked difference in society's attitude towards left-handed and right-handed people. In graphology, there are differences to be seen in the writing of left-handed and right-handed people, so it is interesting to look briefly at how we perceive those differences.

For some reason, left-handed people have always been treated as inferior, even to the point of being regarded as sinister or evil in some societies. The very word 'sinister' is, in fact, Latin for left, but through the years a pejorative connotation has been put upon the word and, even now, there are still some people who regard left-handedness as in some way a deviation from the norm.

However, personal experience has shown that many left-handed people have some special gift or unusual talent of one kind or another. What's more, it takes a lot of adjustment and much strength of purpose for a naturally left-handed person to learn to live in a predominantly right-handed world. Perhaps because of that, left-handed people often react quite speedily in a crisis or emergency. To cope with all the ups and downs of day-to-day living and most of the problems that right-handed people normally take in their stride, left-handed people have had to hone their own personal responses to a slightly higher degree of efficiency than right-handed people.

In the earliest civilisations, however, the ancients took a different view. The left hand has always been associated with evil, wrong-doing, bad luck and so on, so the right hand has naturally assumed the more dominant role and has certainly always been the better favoured. This has been emphasised in the holy scriptures of many different religions. There are a number of references in the Bible to left- and right-handedness, usually associating the right with might and good, and the left with deceit and weakness. However, the first two clear references to left-handedness to be found in the Old Testament are in Judges 3, 15 where a statement refers to Ehud, the son of Gera, as 'a left-handed man', although it does not qualify why he should be referred to in such a way. Later, in Judges 20, 15 and 16, is the most widely publicised statement on the subject, that all of the 700 chosen men from the tribe of Benjamin were left-handed and expert sling shots 'who never missed'. In spite, or perhaps because, of being left-handed, all were considered to be the best fighting men of the area. It was noted that, when being chosen, each man had clearly demonstrated his readiness for battle for none of them was seen to put down his weapons at any time – even when resting. This special force were held in such high esteem that there are legends in several countries that hold all present-day left-handers to be the direct descendants of this tribe.

Early Egyptian religious writings refer to the disparity between the left and right hands. Buddhism affirms that the right-hand path is the true way to Nirvana while the left is, quite simply, the wrong way. Even the Mayan and Aztec religions embraced similar beliefs.

At the turn of the twentieth century, it was estimated there were about seven to eight million left-handed people in Britain alone, or just under six per cent of the total population. A hundred years later, that figure has increased to just under ten per cent of the population, although this may be a statistical anomaly accounted for by the fact that parents and teachers used to make active efforts to 'correct' a child who was naturally left-handed by forcing them to use the right hand. Inevitably, this created a negative psychological effect on the child, who constantly had to override their natural instincts. In some cases, this could even have led to a behavioural imbalance that manifested itself in a stammer or left-slanting (backward) handwriting, which is a clear sign of withdrawal.

A good example of this, in the United Kingdom, was King George VI, who was naturally left-handed, and had to contend with efforts to make him use his right hand more during his childhood. It is thought that this probably resulted in his stammer, a problem he never overcame. However, in the early 1970s, the Scottish Council for Research in Education backed some limited research on changed handedness and concluded that it does not always result in stuttering.

In contrast, HRH Prince Charles, the present Prince of Wales, who is naturally left-handed, was allowed to follow his natural writing instincts. Bad luck prevailing, he had other problems to cope with when he broke his left arm during a polo match. He had to manage with his right hand until his left arm healed sufficiently for him to return to normal. Graphologists at the time looked with interest at the comparison between his normal, left-handed signature and the temporary, right-handed one he was forced to use while his left arm was out of action.

There seem to be no clear-cut reasons why some of us should be left-handed and some of us right-handed, although the predominance of right-handedness seems to be directly related to the development of our intelligence.

The left side of the brain controls the right side of the body, including, of course, the right hand, and whether a person writes with their right or left hand, the right is normally acknowledged to be the dominant hand. The left side of the brain is known as the master hemisphere and is usually more developed than the right side. This is the case whether a person is right-handed or left-handed. The left side controls and defines our judgement and intelligence and two extremely important features of cognition, those of reading and writing, are located in the left hemisphere of right-handed people. In the natural left-hander, this situation is reversed.

Even though this is the case, it is not true to say that left-handedness can be associated with slow perception or a poor intelligence for, generally speaking, the majority of left-handed people are extremely bright and perceptive. Remember, they have had to learn to live in a right-handed world and, as a result, are usually very quick on the uptake.

Most people favour either their left or their right hand. A few people are ambidextrous, although even they rarely use both hands with equal ease. They will be better doing some things with one hand rather than the other although there may perhaps be less difference between the skill with which they can use either hand for particular tasks. For example, even most ambidextrous people prefer to write or draw holding the pen with either their left or their right hand; few use both hands with the same facility. When throwing, many who normally favour their right hand will find the left hand more comfortable to use or will use the left hand when they use an instrument such as a sports racket.

People who are naturally right- or left-handed, on the other hand, find it very difficult to use the other hand. For a right-handed person, using scissors or a toothbrush with their left hand is very difficult, as is using a knife and fork in the opposite hands from usual – it feels very strange and the person will not be able to control the utensils to the same degree. Interestingly, using a spoon tends to present fewer problems, and many people can and do use both hands with equal facility, often without realising it. Sweeping, or just holding a broom with the 'wrong' hand at the top can also create an odd feeling of awkwardness, as can trying to remove a lid from a box or jar using the 'wrong' hand.

Since most people are right-handed, the majority of parents tend to assume that their children will be right-handed until it is proved to the contrary. Once the child starts to reach out and grasp objects, or to use a spoon or fork, they will tend to offer toys or other objects to the right hand, or place the spoon on the right. From observation, however, it will gradually become clear which hand the child tends to favour, and the parents can respond accordingly. If they try to force a young child to use the hand which they do not naturally select, the child may appear slower to learn or respond to a particular activity. It is far better to let the child be the guide.

When you examine handwriting for left-handedness, you look to see how the stroke has been created. When held under a strong magnifying glass, the grain of the stroke looks as though it may have been made in reverse, that is from right to left rather than from left to right. T-bar crossings and dash-style i-dots are often made this way in the writing of a left-hander.

While most right-handed people tend to hold their pen and write in a similar way, left-handed people write in one of two main styles. They may hook their left arm curled round so that their hand is above the writing but with the hand and pen tilted toward the body. This style is known as the 'hook', when the writer pulls the pen across the page; this is the more common left-handed writing style. Alternatively, the writer pushes the pen across the page.

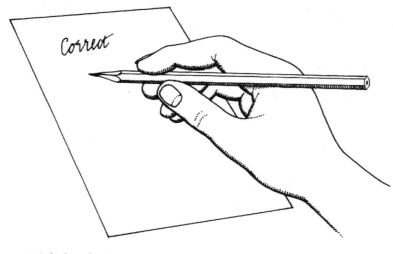

Correct right-hand grip

Whichever style the writer adopts, any problems they encounter will be considerably alleviated if they hold the pen very slightly higher up the barrel than they might normally do. Simply raising the hand's hold on the barrel of the pen a few centimetres higher, will immediately help them to achieve an easier and more fluid and better-controlled path of the pen over the paper. This will help prevent them from smudging their work and, of course, they will be far better able to see what they have just written, allowing them to concentrate more fully on what they are writing.

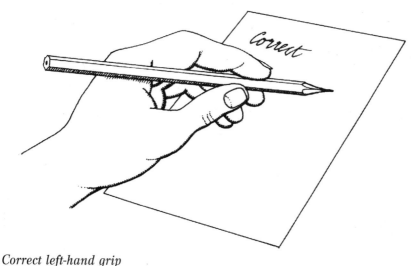

Correct left-hand grip

Many left-handed writers adopt a backward slope to their script because this is so much more natural to perform with the left hand. A left-handed slant can suggest withdrawal in a right-handed person, whereas in handwriting written by a left-handed writer this does not follow, as left-handed writing will tend to lean naturally to the left in many cases. It is therefore essential that the graphologist is aware of this from the start.

Left- or right-handedness is important in handwriting and affords an unerring indication as to how a person can react or behave in an emergency or under stress, the left-hander tending to have the advantage in terms of speed of response, as previously explained. This also means that they are often regarded as more alert, brighter and more perceptive than their right-handed counterparts. On those occasions when you do come to analyse the writing of a left-handed person, therefore, make sure you take this into account when you are assessing features of the script and never underestimate them.

Chapter 5

MARGINS

M argins have a special significance in graphology. Most people do not take deliberate care to lay out their work to allow even and accurate margins; it tends to be the case that only artistic people consider the impression the margins around their writing will make on the reader. However, the fact that we usually form them unconsciously means that a great deal can be learned by examining them from a graphological point of view.

A writer's margins act as a frame around their writing. Therefore, when you first look at a sample of writing on a sheet of paper, try to look at it as though it were a picture. The handwriting is the subject matter, while the margins are the border. As with any type of border, it should be evenly spaced, pleasing to the eye and well placed. An inappropriate, badly made or ill-proportioned frame around a picture detracts from the overall effect. The same is true of badly formed margins around a letter or piece of writing.

The way a writer creates the margins reveals much about their social attitudes and how they tend to react to the world around them. Margins are said to represent the environment in which the writer lives, and to be a reflection of their relationship with their surroundings and the people in them.

Equal margins

Four well-drawn margins, equally balanced and pleasing to the eye, suggest a writer who is comfortable with their lot in life. When a writer fits into their milieu in such a way, it must also follow that they are content, socially accepted and emotionally mature. The same sense of balance and evenness of perception are reflected in their life as in the presentation of their written work. They are also likely to demonstrate good organisational abilities, as these skills can also be implied by the way they set out their handwriting.

Wide top margin

If the top margin is wide and generous, the writer may be rather informal in their manner and prefer friends and partners to take the initiative in decision-making as they do not like making the first move. Perhaps a slight lack of confidence could cause this person to lose out on opportunities, especially in the emotional stakes, through not being sufficiently decisive to snap them up when they arise.

Wide bottom margin

When the lower margin is very wide, this shows that the writer has a fear of their emotions. They may have been hurt or rejected in the past and remain frightened of becoming too involved with other people in case the same thing happens again. Standing on the sidelines often indicates that the writer is lonely and needs to mix and socialise more. Their character is also likely to be intuitive, perceptive and they are probably a good listener.

Wide right-hand margin

Sensitive, highly strung and apprehensive about the future, the writer who leaves a wide right-hand margin is not an easy person to get to know. A one-partner type, this person usually stays with the same person, more often than not for keeps. A rather serious nature means they do not thrive in crowds but prefer to be with a few close friends rather than mixing in large groups.

Narrow right-hand margin

Extrovert and socially adaptable, this writer likes the bright life and being with people. As a rule, the energy levels are good, for this is the type that enjoys or will take part in many activities. They dislike being alone with no one to talk to.

Narrow top margin

There is a directness of approach both to life and love that can bypass convention. There is a dislike of detail. This writer does not play according to the book. They tend to go straight for what they want, when they want it. There is nearly always more than a just a little hint of aggression in their make-up.

Wide left-hand margin

This indicates generosity and extravagance; this writer is likely to make flamboyant gestures and give surprise gifts to friends. No one boosts their partner's ego better than this type for they are fully aware of their own worth and capabilities both in their mental and emotional aspirations. The past holds little interest for these people; they are concerned with the present and the future.

Narrow left-hand margin

Writers who create a narrow left-hand margin tend to be cautious and somewhat inhibited in their approach to life and may be afraid of making mistakes. They can be suspicious and have a tendency to retreat into a corner at times. They need lots of reassurance from those around them that they are wanted and secure.

Wide all-round margin

This suggests a writer who builds walls against intrusion from outside, and this kind of voluntary isolationism can result in the loss of friends. This kind of writer has very little desire to mix and socialise with other people, which means that the writer misses out on personal happiness and emotional satisfaction as a result. This style of margin, however, does often indicate a strong sense of colour and good taste.

No margins

This writer tends to be too thrifty to let go and have a good time. If the margins are virtually non-existent, the person could be putting too much away for a rainy day – and that would include their emotional responses. They should make sure this economical streak does not become too obsessional.

Irregular margins

Irregular margins indicate a love of travel and adventure with a certain amount of restlessness, alternating with a streak of reserve. A writer like this tends to exhibit a rather ambivalent social attitude: one moment extroverted and full of life but the next introverted and inwardly lonely. This can be quite confusing for those around this person.

Widening left-hand margin

Occasionally, the left-hand margin appears to widen gradually as the writer proceeds down the page. This symbolises the optimist, the impatient type who must get things done, quick to pay their own way and over-generous with gifts or life's little luxuries. Economics may be just a word to this type.

Narrowing left-hand margin

When the left-hand margin becomes progressively narrower towards the bottom of the page, the writer is particularly concerned with economy. Writers like this have an in-built caution once a project of any kind gets under way. They take the time to stop and plan properly and leave precious little room for error; they do not like to make mistakes or be seen to do so either.

Widening right-hand margin

A widening right-hand margin indicates a writer who will start things without thinking through what is required. They tend to be rather shy and there may be some reserve; they do not push themselves forward enough and, consequently, can find that they miss out on opportunities. They are likely to worry too much about future events.

Narrowing right-hand margin

This indicates the type who starts almost everything with a considerable degree of reserve but, after all the initial preamble of whatever is involved, tends to come out of their shell and join in more with what is going on. If the sample of handwriting runs to several pages and all the right-hand margins are consistent, it implies that the writer applies too much control, and this should be supported by the assessment of the rest of the script. This suggests strong personal controls, inflexibility, formality and a need to do everything by the book.

Chapter 6

SPACING

When considering the spacing of a piece of writing, the graphologist needs to examine the spacing both around the letters and between the lines, and also the width of the letters themselves. The best way to measure letter width is to look at the letter n. In an average script it should should look square; in narrow writing it will look as if it has been compressed, while in a broad, open script it will be stretched and appear wide.

As a person writes a letter, they unconsciously represent themselves on the page. So, if we take this analogy a stage further, we assume that if the handwriting is narrow or cramped it follows that the writer thinks this way and that they are likely to be narrow-minded and have a critical nature. If the handwriting is wide and expansive, therefore, it must be equally safe to expect the writer to be generous and broad-minded. This writer would tend to be more natural and outgoing. And clearly, there is every degree in between!

As always in graphology, consider all the various elements before you draw any conclusions. You also need to check for speed and the pressure used when looking at the word and letter spacing.

Spacing between letters

The way the writer creates spacing between letters indicates how they like to relate to other people. If they are naturally cautious, then the spacing between individual letters will appear narrow and cramped. Extroverted or outgoing types, on the other hand, will create wide letters with large spaces between them.

When wide spaces are made between letters written in a cramped or narrow style, it suggests the writer makes every effort to appear happy and sociable in public, although in reality, they are likely to be inwardly unsure and somewhat reserved when expressing their real feelings. The reverse of this, narrow spaces within a wide script, indicates a presumptuous character. This person is basically selfish and wants everything their own way. The same does not apply to those dealing with this kind of writer; they must not overstep the mark.

Well-balanced spacing

The spacing between words and lines reveals whether the state of mind of the writer is erratic or orderly, that is whether or not they have clear or muddled thinking.

Well-spaced handwriting with words at an equal distance is an indication of mature thinking. This person has the ability to assimilate emotional experiences and maintain their integrity. It also shows good organisational ability and a well-developed planning capacity.

Good, clear spacing between the lines confirms and strengthens the assessments made if the handwriting has clear, even spacing between letters. It indicates clarity of thought; a writer with well-spaced handwriting can plan well, is orderly and reasonably conventional.

Really well-balanced spacing should always appear equal between lines and words, showing self-assurance and a liberal mind with the faculty of discrimination and social confidence. The example of clear spacing given below shows excellent judgement and a sound organisational ability. The writer is able to discriminate in their intellectual and emotional life. Their social attitude is easy, comfortable and confident.

weather this week w.
that I work in this pa

The average-sized spacing in the next sample widens as the writer continues the letter, revealing an inconsistent personality.

However, when handwriting has almost machine-like, over-controlled spacing between letters, words and lines, then the writer is expressing too much control in their need to ensure that they are never seen in a poor light. These people are born worriers and may adopt a defensive and self-protective attitude.

Wide spacing

If there are wide spaces between words in broad handwriting, the writer will be an extremely selfish type who needs to be in the centre of everything all the time. If there are circle i-dots, expect to find a lot of exaggeration in their dealings (see also page 94). Should the writing also be slightly angular, the writer will exhibit sarcasm and bitterness.

Wide spaces between the lines reflect inner turmoil. The writer dislikes too much social intercourse. They do not trust easily, either because of their own inability to come to terms with what they expect from a relationship or because they have inflated ideas of their own importance. Very large spaces between lines and words and also be a sign of isolation. The writer may feel cut off emotionally and be unable to communicate with others. This style may also indicate a degree of snobbishness, where the writer is aloof and egotistically 'detached and is lacking in spontaneity.

The large spaces between the lines and words in the following sample show an intelligent mind but a somewhat aloof individual who enjoys a certain amount of personal privacy. This writer prefers not to mix socially unless there is real need to do so. Such writers are often artistic or creative and seek a degree of solitude in which to work, regulating their sociability to their requirements.

Narrow spacing

This rigid script with its non-existent or very narrow spacing indicates an obsessive and introverted personality. There is a lack of conformity in the spacing which suggests the writer is inhibited and unable to live an active, socially integrated life.

Small spaces between words in a cramped and narrow script shows a dependent personality. The writer of the sample below is hardly able to think for themselves, let alone be supportive of anyone else. This type needs others to help them organise their lives and can be finicky and full of inhibitions.

Very small spaces between lines indicate a need for the writer to make contact and have the constant companionship of others. If the script also has narrow spacing, as below, the writer may feel insecure and want to become more involved at an emotional level.

Irregular and poor spacing

Poor spacing of lines and words reveals emotional instability, with impulses ruling the intellect. This may indicate a 'grasshopper' mind, jumping from one thing to another without order or method.

Highly irregular spacing between the letters, words and lines is indicative of no control at all. The writer suffers from fluctuating moods, and may be quite sociable one minute and then uptight and withdrawn the next.

Tangled lines, where writing on one line interferes with that on another, suggests a confused and impractical mind: a person who cannot plan or think ahead too clearly. The writer may be sociable, affable and get along with everybody but is likely to suffer from a lack of sense of direction or purpose in life.

The spacing in the next example is almost non-existent. The text is confused: each word and line is a jumbled mess. The writer is unable to think clearly and has difficulty in holding back emotional energy that demands release. There is little discipline, yet the speed of the writing is quite fast, implying an intelligent mind, but one that lacks an ability to check spontaneous impulses.

Thread-like strokes joining words reveal a mentally agile thinker but one who may skip over details in their haste and impatience. The writer is clever at solving problems but can be inclined to manipulate and shows a strong tendency to be impetuous.

Chapter 7

CONNECTIONS

The way a writer joins together, or connects, letters while they are writing is very important in graphology and can tell us more about the individual in terms of their fundamental personality. The four basic forms of connections in handwriting analysis are known as arcade, angular, garland and thread.

Arcade handwriting

In arcade handwriting, the letters are joined almost in an arch movement. The writing can sometimes even look like a series of arches as if composed entirely of the small letter m.

w much you can

me one from just 1

their handwritin

rds to be very c

guess that shows

Arcade writing indicates a person who is hard to know well and who hides behind a rather formal attitude and a degree of social conventionality. There is a lack of ease in the arcade script which stresses form and manner, both socially and aesthetically, but it rarely discloses the writer's inner life. Despite their shyness, however, this writer is often kind.

An individual with this style of writing is likely to possess a creative streak. The higher the arcade is made, the more likely the writer is to be artistic. Many people in the arts, and especially those involved in music, have such formations in their small letters n and m.

Very shallow arcades belong to the schemer who would sham for their own ends; this is someone who feigns amiability in order to deceive others.

Emotionally, the arcade writer may be isolated or reserved and yet have depth of feeling concealed beneath a calm and impenetrable attitude. Arcade writing indicates an inner independence with a profound structural sense, caution and even secretiveness at times. Alert and watchful, arcade writers are frequently mistrustful and test their friendships before acceptance. A certain formality may check spontaneity in relationships and, if the arcades are narrow, they can reveal a degree of inhibition.

Angular handwriting

Angular handwriting is rigid, controlled and disciplined, showing that the writer can find it hard to adapt and is rather inclined to be uncompromising. These strokes also show a firm, determined and sometimes quarrelsome disposition. Unyielding, sometimes even hard, this writer allows the head to rule the heart.

Please find enclose
Readings, with relevan

I also enclosed a quest
Reading), and a lang

We hope to hear fro

Because angular handwriting involves a disciplined movement, it could mean the writer refuses to adapt or has great difficulty when it comes to compromising, often in the belief that firmness is all. It shows persistence and a rather rigid, controlled personality, usually strong-minded but often defensive. The writer is usually unyielding and determined, and has a restrictive attitude but with fixed ideas and opinions. When the writing is angular and extremely regular, it can reveal a stern nature and a sense of obligation that is sometimes without tolerance or humour. More reliable than gracious, angular writers may be aggressive and suspicious, occasionally seeking to impose their will on others.

When the writing is angular and irregular, it can show misguided resolution and extreme stubbornness, possibly stemming from some inner conflict.

Garland handwriting

Garland-style writing can look like a series of bowls, as if composed entirely of the small letter w. This style is usually found in a feminine script.

Garland writing is easy to perform and shows adaptability and a basically non-aggressive personality. Garland writers are receptive and responsive to emotion and tend to be sympathetic to others. They are approachable and usually enjoy a natural spontaneity.

Often, this writer will take the line of least resistance and can lack drive and push, particularly in the area of job or career. Although the writer may be confident and socially responsive, there is a slight tendency under conflict or pressure to lack firm discipline and be easily led by a stronger personality. This may be because garland writers seek to avoid conflict and have a more easy-going nature than people with one of the other styles of connecting stroke. While appealing in their relaxed attitude, this may lead to an indecisive quality about them. They can be fickle and irresolute which makes them seem more dependent than they are.

Because garland handwriting is an almost effortless motion, it is thought by some to reveal laziness, but this is not always so, especially if there are occasional angles in the script.

If garlands are made with some pressure, they denote warmth and an increased vitality. When they are light and broad, they imply that the writer is generous. Flat, weak-looking garlands show a good-natured and compassionate personality with a susceptibility to outside influences.

Thread handwriting

Thready writing is characterised by a thin, wispy quality, the script often tailing off at the end of words into, literally, threads. Thread handwriting can be quite difficult to analyse because of its formation: it is inclined to dissolve into a line.

> *I would like to find out more about my personality. I'm female, 43 years old. I enclose a large stamped self-addressed envelope and hope to hear from you soon. I also enclose*

As a rule, most thread writers are quite quick-thinking individuals with a considerable talent for manipulating and not a little skill in understanding the motives of others. It is often found in the writing of opportunists and those who are skilled in evading responsibilities.

Most thread writing is found in those who have had a reasonable education. It is rare for an uneducated person to have thread writing as it requires speed of thought and fluency of mind.

However, as this type of script is also an indication of a clever and versatile mind, such writers are likely to be intuitive and able to influence people.

Thread writing can lack clarity and, quite often, this means the writer tends to be adaptable but at the cost of having no clear course of action. This infinite linkage of letters often reveals a multiplicity of talents, even creativity. Such writers are highly observant and receive their impressions from everywhere around them. Their intelligence is combined with intuition and perception, so much so that they frequently disregard established forms of behaviour.

They are ready for any situation and are clever at extricating themselves from difficulties, employing an evasive strategy in order to gain their own ends. Thread writers are often involved in the arts or in creative areas where their mental agility and versatility can take them to the top of their profession.

Some thread writers who use, or have, poor pressure are liable to avoid strong or complex situations by side-stepping issues. Very heavy pressure denotes the writer who dislikes routine and who refuses to be chained down by traditional rules and regulations. They feel they must be free to follow their own ideas and instincts.

When thread writing slopes upwards and to the right, it reveals optimism and a well-developed social sense, enabling the writer to mix and communicate with ease.

A word of warning: many confidence tricksters tend to employ this style for they are opportunists who know exactly how, where and when to turn their accomplished dishonesty to account. They cannot be pinned down easily for they are eloquent, plausible and rapid-thinking.

Chapter 8

THE THREE ZONES

Handwriting may be divided into three zones or areas: the upper, middle and lower zones. Every letter occupies at least one of these zones. The letter f is the only trizonal letter as it enters all three of these zones; this is dealt with in the section on the lower zone.

Each of the three zones has a particular aspect of personality and character attributed to it. The more one zone is emphasised, the more the characteristics associated with it are emphasised or predominate in the writer's personality. This is always the case when a letter invades a zone with which it is not normally associated.

How individual letters are composed invariably gives a strong indication of how well the writer tends to cope with their everyday life in terms of their environmental and personal partnerships. This can also include their occupational and social relationships.

The upper, middle and lower zones of handwriting

The three zones reveal whether we are dealing with a person who is basically idealistic and a perfectionist or one who is straightforward and realistic. Personal maturity is reflected in the proportions of the upper and lower zones to the middle zone. Maturity is shown by a proper balance between high and low, reason and intellect. This balance expresses a genuine organiser. Overemphasis of one zone over another indicates a one-sidedness which may signify a weakness in the person's character. However, the underemphasis of a zone may be equally revealing, so the neglected areas also deserve examination.

The upper zone

The letters principally involved when we discuss the upper zone are b, d, f, h, k, l and t, for they are all normally expected to occupy the upper zone.

Some purists suggest the lower case letter i should be included here because of its dot. Strictly speaking they may be right, although I think it is more revealing to deal with the letter i separately (see page 94).

The upper zone reflects and symbolises meditation, abstraction and speculation, unfettered by material considerations. It shows a striving towards idealistic qualities: imagination, vision and seeking after perfection. It is, therefore, linked with the super-ego (conscience and self-criticism). When a script emphasises the upper area to the detriment of the other two zones, there is a lack of practicality in the writer's overall attitude and approach to life.

If the ascenders, that is the upper loops, are written in a more or less conventional way, the writer enjoys run-of-the-mill aims and desires. Any emphasis placed on the more ideological side of the nature is straightforward and will usually conform to an accepted norm. The writer's outlook is that of a realist, sensible and balanced.

When the upper loops are stressed more than the middle zone letters, the personality will be almost entirely concerned with mental and imaginative pursuits. People who write in this style tend to be dreamers and idealists who are often out of touch with reality.

If the ascenders are small, it indicates that the writer finds it difficult to use their initiative and they are likely to be less ambitious than average. The writer may have plenty of common sense and be full of good ideas but there may be a lack of attention to detail. The writer may be unable to put their theories into practical application.

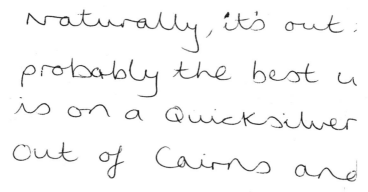

Extremely small ascenders suggest a controlled imagination with a strong element of caution. Such writers tend to concentrate on everyday matters because they will not allow themselves to indulge too much in the realms of fancy or imagination.

The middle zone

The middle zone letters, those without ascenders or descenders, are a, c, e, m, n, o, r, s, u, v, w, x and sometimes z. These letters, which are normally written without upper or lower zone loops, indicate how the writer reacts to everyday matters. The middle zone reflects and symbolises the balance between our cultural and instinctive desires and also indicates a writer's rational social conscience and associated sentiments. Further, it is a measure of the adaptability to everyday reality and the social attitudes of the writer.

When the middle zone is emphasised, the writer is out to impress others. These people like to be noticed, to be at the hub of things. This can lead to them becoming domineering and really rather selfish if this is necessary for them to attain their own ends. The more the middle zone dwarfs the upper and lower zones, the more strongly these traits will be emphasised. This writer only lives for the present, for the past has gone and the future holds no fears.

Ellen's classes finished at ha
and in the abandoned echo
she began to rearrange the
of farmyard animals, the la

In spite of this, however, they may not be overly materialistic. They are basically unconcerned with making or retaining money and assets except for their immediate needs. Their real need is continually to impress those around them and they can do this quite easily without having to use possessions.

Should the middle zone dwarf the lower zone letters, it suggests a somewhat superficial outlook. The instinctive nature is likely to be weak; in some cases it may be overridden completely. These writers are good social animals, capable and confident, but can be hard to get to know on an intimate level.

The world is bundled up in this room. Be
is, where the roads are, we shall be. w
when we go and sling the sun under c
late. I don't know if this is a happy endu

Handwriting which appears to exist almost entirely in the middle zone indicates the practical and down-to-earth type of personality. People who write in this style often have plenty of stamina for the daily grind. They will display a high degree of sound commonsense and usually enjoy good physical health. They tend to have few hang-ups and many have a keen business sense. One

Say Roughly 50 v
I hope you can Re
Never mind Dech

possible difficulty may be in the area of romantic or sexual life, as a tendency to be unable to sustain relationships is characteristic here, so their close or intimate relationships may be unsatisfactory.

The lower zone

The letters involved in the lower zone are g, j, p, q, y and, depending on style, z. Also, the letter f enters the lower zone and is referred to in this category. The lower zone signifies the subject's more instinctive desires, their sexual and physical drive, sports interests, possessiveness and materialism.

This is the sphere of primitive instincts or irrationality. The material demands of self-preservation are found here as well as submerged emotions, sexual tendencies and habits.

Handwriting that emphasises the lower zone refers to those who set much store by possession and material achievement. While this may be viewed by some as a failing, many people who write like this work very hard indeed to achieve their ambitions.

When the descenders are very full or overemphasised, the basic appetites will be accentuated. As a rule, these writers are only interested in physical or outdoor activities. Their sex drive is strong and they are likely to be quite materialistic.

Letters with lower extensions or loops that are so long that they become entangled with the script on the line below, as shown at the top of the next page, denote a lack of order and judgement. These people seem unable to think clearly and logically; their lives are often quite disorganised. They muddle through, often lurching from one problem to the next.

intuition to analyze
of script, but with
experience he or she
able to predict a

Wide bases or triangulated loops suggest an argumentative type, contentious and easily aroused. The writer is quite likely to suffer from sexual frustration or incompatibility. Such a writer may often be something of a tyrant in the home and it is not unknown for such people to be socially aggressive because of disappointment with their partner.

to get any help

The longer this type of loop, the more the writer will exhibit a tendency to exaggerate. They may also be impulsive, rash and self-opinionated. Writers like this will often oppose anything new in their lives, often without even giving the matter proper constructive thought.

A lack of loops or straight lines in the lower zone suggests good judgement for there is an equivalent economy of expression. The writer can be slightly moody but not that easily swayed. This style of writing suggest a connection with musical or mathematical ability.

You will find more information on this topic in Chapter 21.

Other indications

Occasionally, an upper or lower zone extension, either a loop or a straight line, seems to be broken or not properly formed. This can mean the writer has a faulty or missing limb. Such a formation can also occur during temporary illness.

Chapter 9

LEGIBILITY

The need for legible handwriting is, of course, obvious. As a means of communication, whatever else it may represent, the message must be readable so that whoever looks at it can clearly understand what is written. At school, children learn to write in a clear and legible script and the importance of writing neatly and legibly is stressed throughout their schooling. Even with the increased used of word processors and computers, it is important to be able to write clearly, and many people still prefer to write letters by hand, especially personal letters, as they consider, quite rightly, that the effect created by a handwritten letter is different from that created by a letter printed by a computer.

However untidy the handwriting, most people automatically correct any deficiencies in the writing when they are reading a handwritten letter. If a letter is not properly formed or one is missing from a word, the reader will easily understand the meaning. This can, however, create a situation where people read what they 'think' is written on the paper. They read quickly and can often fail to read the message properly. It is quite possible to read what you expect to see rather than what you actually do see.

Illegible handwriting

An illegible script shows carelessness and mistrust, sometimes insincerity, and a general lack of co-operation. Handwriting like this always reflects poorly on the writer as the reader has little alternative but to assume the writer is not sufficiently considerate to ensure that the writing can be understood. A writer should not automatically assume that whatever they have written will necessarily be understood by the recipient. It is up to the writer to make sure of this by presenting a neat and clearly formed script. If it is illegible, the failure in communication is their responsibility

Sometimes bad handwriting is considered a result of the writer's profession. It is a standing joke that doctors have illegible handwriting, perhaps stemming from a notion that only fellow professionals and other colleagues who share the same knowledge will read the writing, and they will be able to decipher it. It may also have been a way, perhaps unconsciously, of concealing secrets from those whom they think should not read the notes – such as the patients.

When other people need to interpret the communications, however, it becomes a different story. Some graphologists interpret this kind of illegible script in a positive way as showing a degree of confidentiality, discretion, flexibility and intuition, combined with a desire for freedom of action, but in a slightly restricted area. This kind of interpretation, however, must be treated with caution. Fortunately, a more enlightened view of the need for doctor–patient communication and also the use of computers has mitigated the effects of bad handwriting amongst doctors.

Legible handwriting

Legible script must not be mistaken for decipherable handwriting for they are not precisely the same. Legibility means that every word is absolutely clear and easily understood even when a letter, word or phrase is taken out of context. Decipherable handwriting indicates that the communication can be fully understood without too much effort, even though there may be the occasional unclear word, missing or poorly formed letter, or other slight confusion. The context of the letter overcomes any such difficulties.

Those whose work requires meticulous attention to detail are more likely to present a clear and uniform script than colleagues involved in more creative activities.

Since i don't have a clue what to do
take some sentences from the magazine
"The lantern is a memorial to Jack
Irish villain who was so nasty that

A legible script reveals sincerity and purposefulness, a careful attention to detail, clear communication and comprehension. The legible script, however, can also be a sign of convention, and even pedantry if taken to extremes. Writers with excessively neat handwriting may dislike breaking the rules. They prefer to play the game straight and can, as a result, be quite boring. Over-precise handwriting also indicates a lack of impulse, vision and foresight. This kind of writer can have a rather narrow outlook and will rarely be capable of true originality.

When you come to assess clarity or legibility of a script you must remember that a clear and well-presented letter shows an organised and uncluttered mind. When you cannot understand what is written, the writer does not care very much for your opinion, preferring only their own. In any terms, that attitude is rude and ignorant.

Chapter 10

PRESSURE

O ne of the principal advantages of collecting several samples of the handwriting of one person over a period of time is that they show variations of mood and fluctuations of temperament in the writer. When only one sample is available, it becomes rather difficult to define the overall mood and vitality; we have to rely entirely on what we have in front of us – and that will only show the mood of the writer at the time of writing.

Periods of stress, carefree moments, the writer's current physical health and emotional upheavals all have a bearing on how they will shape their script at any given time. Therefore, the pressure or speed of the sample will also furnish clues to the subject's health and mood only at the time of writing.

The intensity of mood and vitality is measured by the amount of pressure exerted on the page. Few people realise how heavily they apply pressure on the paper as they write because it is almost always a subconscious action.

A fountain pen or felt-tip pen will show how much pressure the writer has exerted on the paper by the fact that the strokes appear to spread out, creating a 'pasty' or slightly blurred image. Many writers now use a ballpoint pen and in this case, pressure is measured more literally by the impression the pen makes on the paper, rather than the look of the script.

Heavy pressure

Heavy pressure that goes through the paper and makes a deep impression on the other side shows plenty of vitality. The writer is energetic and readily influenced by things they can feel, touch and see. Such writers are the 'doers' of this world. They have a liking for colour, movement, action and a sense of having a goal to aim for – achievement is important to them. Persistent and persuasive, these writers live for today rather than the promise of things to come.

a year's biorhythms – I have unfortunately lost the set rec. received from you.

Heavy pressure, therefore, indicates a healthy libido, endurance and a certain amount of personal strength. Emotional strength and an enthusiasm for life are other positive factors.

However, when heavy pressure is seen in a slowly executed script, the writer's energies are likely to be poorly channelled. The writer may also be a depressed or slightly frustrated character.

Light pressure

Lightish pressure on the paper and a slow speed of writing suggest a controlled emotional personality. These writers are not moody but are much more likely to be consistent, although they may be inclined to be somewhat reserved. When hesitations are seen in this kind of handwriting it implies a temporary delicate state at the time of writing. Once health gets back to par, the script will return to normal.

This suggests you were aware the intentions of the others

Consistently light pressure reveals highly sensitive people who are easily hurt and can be quick to take offence. These people have a strong critical sense; they have a sharp tongue and tend to be sarcastic if under pressure. Encouragement and praise may tone down this sharpness. Because they are reserved and can be rather prickly, they select their close friends with care. These writers go for pastel shades and the lighter side of life. Emotionally, perhaps, they tend to need affection more than sex.

When the pressure is exceptionally light it indicates frequent periods of fatigue with poor reserves of energy. Loyal and conventional, a person who writes in this way can be inclined to distrust new ideas until they have concrete proof that the change is a good one.

Medium pressure

Generally speaking, medium pressure is the most widely found and reflects a reasonably well-balanced personality whose disposition is friendly. These writers get on well with those around them and rarely go to extremes, emotionally or socially. They will not normally make a great show of enthusiasm or go into raptures easily.

The enclosed sample is from a friend asking for help.

They are able to adjust well to the world around them and for the most part are better adjusted than those who exert heavy pressure. They are not too aggressive or ambitious when trying to achieve their aims and they tend to take most things in their stride without getting into a flap. Less impatient and volatile than the heavy-pressure group, they deal with problems using a good balance between mind and emotion.

Intermittent pressure

Script revealing an excessively wide variation in pressure, or executed with very light or very heavy pressure, is always a sign of something wrong with the writer at the time of writing. This may be physical ill health or, more probably, emotional tension or mental stress. In these cases, the writer is unable to control the pen correctly, especially if the script sample appears to be spiky or slants first one way, then another.

[handwriting sample]

Intermittent pressure in a person's handwriting implies unsteady will-power; responses to external stimuli may vary according to the mood of the moment. If the pressure changes intermittently in one single piece of writing rather than over a number of examples, then the unsteadiness is emphasised further. Such a person is not always reliable. They may suffer from inner tensions resulting in some insecurity and inconsistency in the way they behave.

When the writing pressure wavers – sometimes light, sometimes heavy – this is an indication of an erratic personality who possibly suffers from severely changing moods. These writers tend to be unpredictable and often feel under stress. Their feelings tend to fluctuate like the wind and they are rather difficult to pin down to a course of action.

This fluctuating emotional nature can make them hard to deal with or even sometimes to understand. Because they find it hard to establish a routine, their lifestyle can be disordered and may suffer from a lack of harmony and stability.

Chapter 11

STARTING AND ENDING STROKES

Those little strokes at the beginning and end of words reveal what sort of character the writer has, whether they are a quick starter or a cautious individual.

Starting strokes

Lead-in strokes may be used by the writer because that was how they were originally taught to construct their letters. Where and how they were taught to write is therefore very important.

Normally when a writer uses lead-in strokes they are almost always as a sort of prop or support. The writer is showing that they are uncertain, unsure, self-doubting. They may be conventional and like to take their time before making decisions.

If there are no starting strokes, the writer is confident, able to work and use their initiative without worrying unduly about what others might think. If words are begun without a starting stroke, the writer is someone who usually gets down to the essentials rapidly and without too much fuss. They tend to be quick-thinking, like to set goals and achieve them, have an eye for detail and vision for planning ahead.

A very long starting stroke indicates that the writer likes to take their time preparing the way before tackling any new project and that there is more than a hint of caution in their make-up.

Hello

A hook at the beginning of words indicates tenacity of purpose with a rather obstinate nature and firmly held opinions. Such writers are not easily swayed by other people and like to think that they are not influenced by them.

A loop at the beginning of words, as in the example below, is often a sign of jealousy – a small loop shows personal jealousy while a large loop is a sign of professional jealousy. Handwriting with a long angular stroke that starts in the lower zone shows the writer to be aggressive, assertive and egotistical with a well-developed critical sense, but a poor sense of humour because of a lack of tolerance of the supposed faults of other people.

A starting stroke like a small arc means that the writer enjoys talking and likes the sound of their own voice. They need to express their own personality but can be dogmatic and inclined to have some quite fixed ideas and opinions.

Ending strokes

Ending strokes reveal social attitude: whether the writer is open and socially minded or unco-operative. It can also indicate whether they conserve their personal resources or have a tendency to meanness.

A long ending stroke indicates social awareness and generosity, although if the stroke is extended for too long it can also show an intolerant and highly critical nature.

A hook at the end of a word shows egotism and an aggressive or even abrasive nature, with a certain amount of defensiveness, and a fighting spirit that does not like to admit defeat.

this is the

If there is no ending stroke but simply an abrupt halt to the last word, it is a sign of brusqueness. A person showing these tendencies is likely to be able to sever relationships without regret.

Maybe

If the ending stroke reaches upward into the upper zone, the writer may be showing spiritual or religious leanings, or even have an interest in occult matters.

graphology

Should the ending stroke go up and over to the left over the last word, the writer is likely to be patronising to those around them and may also be inclined to be introspective.

take

An enrolled claw at the end of a stroke is always a sign of greed and selfishness, which may originally have been caused by negative experiences in early life.

(then

When the final stroke returns to the left under the last word, it suggests a hot temper and unwillingness to compromise.

they

Chapter 12

SIZE

The size of handwriting is significant because it reveals whether the writer is a person who values thought or emotion more highly. Generally speaking, handwriting should be about 3 mm (⅛ in) high in the middle zone. The same sizes are allowed for descending and ascending strokes or loops into their respective zones. Thus, an overall size of about 9 mm (⅜ in) is the accepted norm while anything larger than this is considered large handwriting and anything smaller is regarded as small script. It is important to remember, however, that there are no hard and fast rules.

Large handwriting

The larger the script, the more likely it is that the writer has a sentimental and affectionate side to their nature, very often accompanied by an emotional impulsiveness that can have unfortunate repercussions at times.

Large letters also indicate how extrovert a person is. The writer who has large handwriting will tend to be more extravagant and extrovert with a strong need to make an impression everywhere they go. Large writing is a sign of someone who needs plenty of space in which to live, work and play. With these people, there is always an urge for self expression, a desire to show off and thereby gain the attention and admiration of all those with whom they come into contact. Such writers are unhappy in restricted or repressive environments or relationships. They always feel the need to demonstrate their love and affection.

The larger the handwriting, the more inclined they are to lack thought; they are bold and reckless and often a little too enthusiastic and optimistic. Attention to detail is not their forte and they can overlook this at the expense of trying to achieve their aim.

Exaggerated and large writing can indicate an obsessional nature, someone who is obstinate and difficult to deal with, one who must have their own way and who rarely considers others. Usually, there is a strong dislike of red tape, or petty bureaucracy because they consider that the rules are made for everyone else – not them!

This huge script with its outsize letter shows an animated, over-zealous personality, a person who is fond of their own way and who possesses an exaggerated ego. The writer finds it hard to concentrate for long periods, is restless and likes to be seen and heard. Extravagant and over-active, there are signs of tension in the heavy pressure which the writer probably aggravates by a dominant and excessively impatient nature.

The handwriting below shows an extremely social-minded personality who is inclined to be over-generous, someone who likes to entertain on a lavish scale and is very much aware of their emotions. They are impatient and easily bored by details; they enjoy plenty of attention, and are basically non-aggressive but egotistical; they are materialistic and somewhat selfish in their attitude.

Small handwriting

Small writing is a sign of intelligence and analytical thinking but the tendency is to allow the head to rule the heart. There is so much caution and responsibility in this writer's nature that it can act as a brake to impulsiveness and spontaneity.

Small script indicates an introspective personality. The writer does not actively seek recognition, although a 'please' and a 'thank you' will make them a devoted fan. They are content to organise, as they often have good executive ability. However, do not be fooled, these people are not exactly the shy and retiring type; they are quite independent and may have a very strong inner power drive.

Very small, almost minute, writing suggests a writer with feelings of inferiority, the type who prefers to hide away from the limelight with no wish to be noticed. These writers may have suffered from emotional upsets, experiences and influences in their early life which they find hard to shake off.

This script with its almost illegible letters indicates feelings of inferiority and a lack of confidence. The writer is afraid of making decisions and reveals a lot of inhibition, both mentally and emotionally. They are incapable of normal socialising because of an introspective nature which has resulted in a natural lack of warmth and feeling. Everything around them is intellectualised, including their emotional needs.

Medium handwriting

As a rule, most handwriting falls between these two extremes. Medium-sized handwriting implies a good balance between the head and heart – between impulse and control. Usually, this kind of writer has the ability to maintain their equilibrium between the senses and the mind. They are adaptable, conventional, practical and realistic.

The medium-sized script overleaf shows a good balance between head and heart. The writer distinguishes well between what is essential and what is not in the social area and enjoys harmony whenever possible. There is no great urgency for self-expression and little evidence of a domineering streak in the overall character structure. This is an average-sized handwriting as used by most people.

Variable letters

When a handwriting has clear evidence of variable letter sizes, expect to find an inconsistent personality, someone who suffers from moods and is easily thrown off balance by events. Such a writer is likely to be childish, petty, selfish and quite immature, although probably not vindictive.

Chapter 13

SLANT

The slant of handwriting indicates whether a writer is forward-looking and adventurous or is instead someone who continually clings to the past.

Inclined script

The most usual handwriting slant is to the right. This indicates an outgoing nature, someone who is sociable and actively goal-minded and full of enthusiasm for the future.

People whose writing slopes to the right are affectionate, sociable and demonstrative types who thrive in company. They have the knack of choosing the right occupation or vocation and of being successful in both business and personal relationships. Relationships are very important for these writers, and are much more meaningful than material things at times. Because they tend to be extrovert, they like to be surrounded by other people so they can bounce off them all their pet ideas, feelings, desires and wishes. On their own, they tend to lose their sense of purpose.

Inevitably, things are liable to go wrong in anyone's life, but these writers have the ability to bounce back reasonably well from any setbacks that life may throw at them.

People whose writing slants to the right tend to let their emotions guide them more than reason – even when it comes to hard decisions – as this writing style is a sure sign of very strong emotional impulses and needs. The instincts are strong and these writers use them to good effect. Actors, nurses, politicians and salesmen all tend to be those who write with a forward slant. It is also common among those who help others come together in groups or organisations.

People in a hurry, the active types who get things done, write this way. The more active the individual, the more their writing is likely to slope to the right. The greater the angle from the vertical, more than 45 degrees, the more impulsive the nature. This is the sign of the enthusiast, the one who tends not to stop to reflect but who prefers to move forward quickly every time they see something that catches their fancy. Because of this, they may also have a slightly over-excitable temperament which can sometimes get out of control, particularly when they are under stress or where their emotions are involved.

Sometimes, in normally forward-sloping handwriting, there may be an extra inclination to the right, especially at the end of the word, sentence or line. This indicates the writer whose personal interest outweighs any reserve that they may have. It suggests hot-headedness and, perhaps, something of a quick temper.

The right slant in the handwriting sample below is an indication of the extrovert nature of the writer and the desire to mix and meet socially. The rounded strokes indicate an affectionate and warm nature, while the speed of the writing denotes someone with a quick-thinking mind.

The quick brown jumped over the

Reclined script

No one teaches a child to write with a backward slant, so it indicates a deviation from the 'norm' in some way.

Handwriting that slants to the left indicates introversion and self-consciousness. If you have a sample with a left slant, the writer has a rather over-active inner life. They may have been heavily influenced by a stronger character a little too early in their formative years and subsequently find it hard to break away from a seemingly ever-present influence. Their confidence in their own individuality may not have fully developed.

There is a certain amount of detachment in the nature of this type of writer and they may often feel isolated and in the minority. This writer puts up barriers as a defensive measure to protect a rather fragile ego. Sensitive, with strong family ties, they are often creative and artistic.

An inbuilt cautionary factor will prevent them from acting spontaneously and therefore make it difficult for them to establish intimate friendships and also to maintain them. In drawing away from people, this writer becomes difficult to get to know intimately. They tend to distrust most overtures towards any kind of relationship and may tend to be suspicious of new faces in either the social or working environment. A cautiousness is certain to be apparent in their dealings with newcomers, whom they are likely to assess in some detail before deciding on whether any level of relationship is appropriate.

Usually, this writer has an incredible amount of inner sensitivity, but sufficient emotional control to conceal their true feelings even from those who like to think they are close to them. This can foster a selfish nature, and this is usually indicated by reclined handwriting, always more so if the writing is angular because then the writer will prefer their own company. This writer likes to think alone, work alone and be alone.

However, should you succeed in breaking down those barriers and making friends, they will become the most loyal of companions, always helpful when you are in any kind of trouble. This person is very best kind of friend – the one who never lets you down. You always need to make sure, however, that you are not the one to be unreliable in your friendship and you must always respect their privacy in order to keep their hard-won trust.

This extreme left slant shows introversion and a strong pull from past experiences. The underlengths indicate a strong maternal influence; wide spacing between words implies emotional isolation.

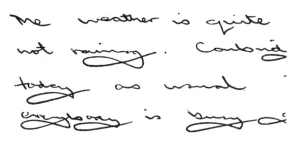

Vertical script

An upright script suggests an independent and self-reliant personality. In children's handwriting this shows good head control even at an early age: the head rules the heart here, and this writer is not easily swayed either by their emotions or by external influences. Poise, and what appears to be a curious lack of empathy, make these writers seem more self-controlled than they actually are.

Basically, the writer of a vertical script tends to be reserved, self-contained and calm. This is the hallmark of a good leader because in a decision-making situation they will always consider all the options carefully, both in terms of their short-term and long-term effects. They do not like to make mistakes, nor be seen to make them.

There are aspects of this person's nature that can be quite off-putting as, no matter how hard you try, this writer does not permit any easy intimacy. Once in a relationship, they tend to like to exert control. Socially, they are slightly reserved. At work, relationships can be difficult for they rarely relinquish control over what is going on in the work environment.

Writers in this style are realists. They do not lack affection or sentiment but they will deliberately avoid showing it. There may be a hint of snobbery in their make-up, too.

If, in a vertical handwriting, the middle zone is large, the writer may be a little more extrovert, a trifle more outgoing than the writer with a smaller middle zone. The former is reliable and reasonable, but the latter will be more critical and reserved.

The upright script below, with its slightly angular strokes, shows good mental and personal control with a certain amount of aggression. The writer is straightforward and intelligent but inclined to keep their emotions in check.

Thirty days hath
April, June + dull

Mixed slants

Handwriting with a mixed slant, one that slopes left, right and even upright for a short while, indicates an erratic disposition and inconsistent personality structure.

A writer with this style is pulled easily in several directions at once and finds it hard to stick with routine. There are often quite strong emotional forces found behind some of their unpredictable actions. Because their emotional and mental natures are likely to fight each other for dominance, it can cause wide variations of mood. As a result they will be impressionable, especially to atmosphere, environment and people.

This erratic handwriting that goes first to the left and then to the right shows inconsistency and belongs to an extremely moody type who has difficulty in sticking to one task. The varying slant and size is often found in the script of people who enjoy plenty of physical and mental activity.

Occasionally handwriting may slant to the right in the middle zone but have reclining upper and lower zone extensions. There is a lot of tension here. Socially, the writer will want to join in but their inner nature will be unwilling. There will be some difficulty in coming to terms with this.

Should the middle zone slant left but both upper and lower extensions swing to the right, the writer does not really want to be one of the crowd but may allow themselves to be dragged along to a social affair now and then and may even enjoy the experience.

it was very kind of
you. I am thinking
about you on your
Birthday.
I am so worried about

Chapter 14

CAPITAL LETTERS

T he use and size of capital letters in a script are useful to an overall handwriting analysis as they are guides to the writer's feelings about themselves and how they express their personality. Medium-sized capital letters show objective valuation of the self, with the obvious changes to that view signified by larger or smaller capitals.

Capital letters

When the capitals are very large, but the script is medium sized, expect to find vanity, pretentiousness and a high regard for the self. The writer dislikes being overlooked and will develop an individual style that will include exaggeration at times.

Flourishes on a capital letter show a big ego and a vulgar form of conceit. Any exaggerated loop on a capital letter is a sign of self-love and superfluous mannerisms.

Broad and large capitals suggest wastefulness and vulgarity, while simple, original capitals imply a high degree of intelligence and originality.

Small capitals indicate concentration, a critical sense and the power to assimilate facts. They can also reveal over-scrupulousness, pettiness and, perhaps, feelings of inferiority.

Narrow capitals imply reserve, shyness and inhibition.

Simple capitals show intelligence, naturalness and sincerity with attendant elimination of non-essentials. The writer may be creative and can distinguish what is important and what is not, but may lack appreciation of anything that does not serve a purpose.

When there are different forms of the same capital letters in one sample of handwriting it is an indication of versatility.

We would look to the capital letter J to determine the drive and enthusiasm of the writer, the larger it is, the more open and balanced the outer personality, probably accompanied by a healthy libido as well.

The smaller the capital letter J, the less this will be so. The writer will exhibit uncertainty when it comes to making decisions. Should they use a dot instead of a cross-bar when writing the capital, there will be some feelings of inferiority. They would prefer to follow rather than lead.

The personal pronoun

The capital I is one of the most important items in handwriting analysis apart from the signature. It shows how the person wishes the world to see them and how they feel about their personal standing in it. The way a person writes the capital I reveals their ego rating and shows how they feel about themselves. Whether the I is large or small, angular or rounded, indicates a lot about personality.

If the capital I is twice as large as the rest of the script, the writer has a fairly healthy ego and a high opinion of themselves, but they could be a little bit too overpowering when placed in a position of authority.

I bought a

On the other hand, a small I shows a person who may have mild feelings of inferiority and does not always assert themselves when they should. They probably need to come out of their shell and let their emotions have free rein now and then.

I have..

A printed capital I indicates a well-balanced personality and an interest in literary matters which could be channelled into a creative sphere. They may also have a general interest in culture and a cultured attitude to life.

I have

A capital I written like the figure 7 or 9 shows that money will be important in the writer's life and they may have a head for figure work. The material things of life are important here as they represent comfort and security.

vv really had maternal feelings
ortant to me – I'm not too good
nutment! I think I've more a
– but I just wondered
any indication from my

A capital letter I looped at the top shows a good sense of humour and an uncomplicated personality. This writer shines at sorting out problems for other people. There is a down-to-earth, common-sense attitude with the ability to cope with the unexpected.

logy report. I am obviously
ale + am 54 years old. I
shortly be moving from this
to Staffordshire. I am
terested in graphalogy +

When the letter I is fragmented at both the top and the bottom, a degree of erratic behaviour or inconsistency will be present in the personality. The past may influence this writer's thinking quite

I'm a thirty one (
of two children an
to learn what you c
about me through
I'm presently emk

markedly. In the formative years, they may have suffered from a lack of environmental security, which now reveals itself in erratic personality traits.

A claw-like capital I with a stroke that goes back towards the left shows a love of material things. The writer may also try to avoid responsibility in their sexual life and be apprehensive about or have difficulty in establishing long-term relationships. This style does, however, indicate a strong sense of family loyalty.

An extremely left-slanting capital I shows a guilt complex and often a difficulty in discussing private emotional problems.

A complicated capital I indicates a high degree of self-awareness. The writer is likely to be wrapped up in their own little world and may even put up barriers against any intrusion. They will not feel much consideration for the needs of others, although there will be plenty of affection in their nature which, if properly channelled into friendships and wider horizons, can make the writer a more sociable and loving person.

A capital I like a capital O indicates a writer who is frequently on the defensive and none too confident. Although the writer enjoys admiration and likes to feel popular, an innate introspective and shy nature holds them back from making friends easily.

Should the letter I be rolled in two loops, it is a sign of self-protection. The writer is a little afraid of the outside world and suspicious of the motives of others. They may have been hurt in previous relationships and need to let go of the past and start afresh.

An angular capital I is a sign of aggression, of someone who likes to be in charge of the home. Arguments in the home now and again add a sense of excitement. A good sense of organisation is also indicated by this style.

A huge, inflated letter I implies someone with an exaggerated ego and a love of spreading themselves around by showing off, giving vent to an innate sense of drama. They love to be the centre of attention and know how to express themselves and be noticed.

A straight, stick-like capital I, as in the example at the top of the following page, is a sign of good judgement and a desire to stick with the essentials. This writer does not like fuss and, although not a romantic, they tend to be fatalistic in their relationships. An intelligent, capable and objective personality (when they want to be), they are able to eliminate the unimportant from important matters and assume responsibility for a wide range of activities when necessary.

Should the small letter i be used as the personal pronoun instead of the capital I, the person will possess little drive. The writer undervalues themselves, may be immature and is very likely to be the sort of person who is easily led.

Chapter 15

LOWER CASE i

The way writers form their i-dots is a very special feature of handwriting analysis as this is only letter, apart from j, that is written first with a stroke and then a dot. While the stem is created as a part of the flow of the script, the dot is made with a free hand – always assuming, of course, the writer uses a dot. As a rule, the majority of writers do make a dot of some kind, and it is the way this mark is made that concerns us here.

The completed letter i, including the stem and the dot, shows how the personality has developed. This includes a writer's attention to detail and efficiency, sense of humour, flexibility, perceptivity, temper, selfishness, sensitivity and loyalty.

The dot of the lower case letter j and cross-bar of the letter t are also made in a free style. The first is discussed on page 162 and the latter dealt with in Chapter 16.

With the letter i, the stem is created during the writing of the whole word but the dot may not be made until the rest of the word is finished. The pen is lifted from this last point and returned to where the writer intends to place the dot. This is not as easy an exercise as it may at first seem and, while it does happen, it is very difficult to stop the pen just where and when we want to, unless a conscious effort is made to do so. To stop in the middle of the flow of handwriting, make the dot and then continue writing can feel uncomfortable.

The positioning of the dot, therefore, is of much more importance than one may at first appreciate. In our formative years, with our teacher's guidance, we begin to develop a personal handwriting style until we reach a fair degree of proficiency. As we progress, we develop a personal and distinctive style all our own; our handwriting soon becomes an unconscious habit. We then pick up speed and, after a little while, modifications to suit or reflect our personal temperament start to creep in. We may add extra elements, adapt others and slowly, steadily, our style develops.

However, whether or not your teacher told you when you first began to write how to make the dot, it is most unlikely that they supervised exactly how, when and where you did it. You would only have known that the i required a dot. As a result, the way a writer makes and places a dot is very much a matter of personal choice and habit and this freedom of movement has taken on a significant importance in analysis.

As it may appear small and insignificant, the i-dot can be easily overlooked, but this is a mistake. As it is written unconsciously, it can be the key to character development, a fact novice graphologists are liable to forget. Dots are particularly interesting when they appear heavy in light-pressure script, or light in a heavy-pressure script. So important are they, that in anonymous letters and forgery the writer can be detected if or when they fail to make the effort to disguise their personal style.

Dot position
A low-set, exactly placed i-dot suggests a precise nature.

A dot placed to the left of the stem shows strong links with the past and a tendency to procrastinate and delay when decisions need to be made. Hesitation is indicated and this can lose the writer opportunities.

An i-dot made to the right of the letter reveals impatience and an ambitious nature. The future, rather than the past, motivates this writer. They are also likely to be impulsive in their dealings.

High-flying dots indicate a daydreamer, one who lacks a firm grasp of reality. A certain amount of hastiness and enthusiasm for new ideas can be present, but the writer will lack the persistence to follow them through.

Dot pressure

Heavy i-dots are a sign of mild depression and weariness. If they are extra heavy in relation to the rest of the writing, they can show anger or frustration, often in the emotional or sexual life of the writer.

Lightly made i-dots suggest sensitivity and, if very weak or non-existent, a lack of physical strength or energy. This writer often has a good critical sense.

Shaped dots

An i-dot like an arc or a comma is a sign of a quick, agile mind and is often found in a person who is active. They may have quite a high level of self-esteem. If the arc is angular, the writer will have a sharp tongue.

Should the i-dot arc to the right the writer will be intuitive and have excellent powers of observation.

An i-dot in the form of a dash shows aggression, temper and a lot of irritability. Clever, but impatient, this writer has little tolerance and does not suffer fools gladly.

The circle i-dot is a sign of immaturity with a sense of drama thrown in. The writer loves the limelight and has an attendant desire for attention. They may be known for a mild or even wild eccentricity in gesture, dress or habit or may even suffer from food fads.

i n

An i-dot connected to the next letter shows a perceptive and very clever mind. The writer has quick reflexes.

l'u

Arrow-shaped dots indicate aggression and hostility with a touch of sarcasm often acting as a defensive measure.

i n

A wavy line for a dot implies a fun-loving character with a sense of humour.

Other indicators

No i-dots at all suggests poor organisational ability, a lack of order and method. The writer may be careless or even absent-minded and is apt to miss details.

When the stem of the letter i is consistently smaller than the rest of the middle-zone letters it indicates introversion with a worrying nature; there is also some inner insecurity. When it is the same size or larger than the the rest of the script, the writer is self-confident and has poise.

Varying i-dots that fluctuate wildly in size and slant within the same sample show an impressionable nature, someone whose opinion and behaviour can vary according to mood or external influences of the moment.

Chapter 16

LOWER CASE t

The lower case letter t is a very special feature in graphological analysis. It is the only letter written with two strokes, one of which is made entirely free hand – if, indeed, the writer uses a cross-bar as the majority of writers do. The dot of the lower case letter i is also made in a free style and this has been discussed fully in Chapter 15.

When the letter t is formed, the stem is created during the flow of writing the whole word, but the horizontal bar may not be made until the rest of the word, or even the sentence, is finished. The pen is then lifted from the paper at this point and returned to where the writer intends to place the cross-bar. Although it does happen, it is very difficult to stop a pen just where and when we want to, unless a conscious effort is made to do so. To stop in the middle of a letter, make the cross-bar and then continue writing is not comfortable.

As a result, the position of the cross-bar takes on a far greater importance than one may first appreciate, in just the same way as the i-dot. When we are learning to write, the teacher does not necessarily supervise exactly how we form the bar across the t, so as we develop our own distinctive writing style and this becomes unconscious, it gradually develops into something which is truly unique. The fact that we were not taught exactly how to place the t-bar means that this becomes a matter of personal choice and habit, making it of enormous importance in analysis. The completed letter t, including the stem and cross-bar, shows how the writer's personality has developed and grown. This will give evidence of characteristics such as the writer's ambitious nature, efficiency, enthusiasm, flexibility, temper, independence, resourcefulness, selfishness and sensitivity.

Certain types of the small t may be be recognised instantly as well-known or accepted stroke formations, but unusual t-bar crossings can put the graphologist at a disadvantage.

T-bar position

A t-bar positioned low down can indicate mild depression. If the stroke is weak, the writer may lack strong will-power. They may find it hard to make decisions and may have a poor sense of responsibility or be unable to take the lead. Care should be taken here, for a weak t-bar can also reveal poor health.

A very highly placed t-bar crossing is a sign of rising ambition and optimism, the desire to achieve aims. When the t-bar is particularly high it could suggest daydreaming on the part of the writer who might live in a fantasy world.

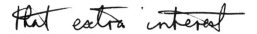

A t-bar that flies to the right of the stem is a sign of a quick, agile mind, of zeal and imagination. There is a need for freedom of action and a dislike of restrictions.

Shaped and sloped t-bars

A hooked t-bar shows a great tenacity of purpose. At the start of the bar it indicates possessiveness; at the end, it implies someone who is critical, perhaps dissatisfied with their lot.

A looped t-bar crossing shows sensitivity and if the stem is also looped this is increased. The writer is easily hurt, overreacts under pressure and becomes anxious as tension builds up.

situation

A t-bar that slopes to the left of the stem is a sign of caution and deliberation. Such writers rarely make impulsive gestures or act spontaneously; everything is carefully thought out because they worry about making mistakes.

t   t   t

A t-bar that slopes down to the right indicates sudden and unexpected anger. These writers have a hasty temper and are extremely obstinate in the face of opposition. They brood and can be rather moody and unpredictable.

kneck with

A straight t-bar of equal length on each side of the stem reveals a good balance between the mind and the emotions. The writer exhibits self-confidence and has steady conscientious attention to detail, but no great dynamic thrust.

obtained, intend to

When the t-bar has a triangular formation, as shown overleaf, it shows an aggressive nature and a lack of tolerance. There will be a swift reaction to any form of rejection or emotional disappointment. This t-bar is frequently found in the writing of those disappointed with their partner.

[handwriting sample]

A heavy, thick t-bar indicates energy and drive, but if the stroke is excessively heavy it shows a domineering personality, one who will not hesitate to use force as an aid to their argument.

to

A sharply pointed t-bar is a sign of a sarcastic and quick-tempered personality. It also denotes an argumentative type, quick to take offence and blame others, perhaps due to an in-built antagonism if their hopes and dreams fail to be realised.

[handwriting sample]

There are well over 250 different ways of making the t-bar. A single sample of handwriting may show a writer may use 10 or 15 variations in the course of a letter, however long the letter may be, and this is perfectly normal.

Take time to compare all the examples of the letter t where it starts a word, sentence or line. Note the style when it is in the middle of a word, next to another small t and at the end of a word, sentence or line. Extreme consistency of construction indicates strong self-control; the writer could be a very difficult person to get to know. When there are mild variations, it shows the writer is quite normal and subject to mild changes of temperament. Wild variations, depending on how different they are, suggest the writer is probably moody, sensitive to atmosphere, colour, noise and people, and easily calmed or stimulated.

Chapter 17

NUMBERS

It is often quite difficult to obtain a reasonable specimen of the way people write numbers because, apart from the date and any numbers in the address, most of us don't use numbers a great deal in our ordinary letters. Despite the fact that we are surrounded by numbers throughout our lives, we tend not to write them a great deal – once we have given up maths lessons. Those who are directly concerned with numbers, either at work or in their hobbies, and therefore write them regularly, are most likely to write numbers clearly and legibly, but this is not always the case.

The way numbers are formed is an outward expression of the writer's inner concern with material matters. The most a graphologist can usually hope for when they are doing a handwriting assessment is the few numbers in an envelope address, on a cheque or a piece of scrap paper, the latter being the best example because it will be in the writer's most natural hand. In fact, it is interesting for a graphologist to compare the writing of normal numbers with those used for money on cheques or bills. These are frequently written larger, denoting a concern with material values.

Position on the page

If a row or list of numbers is written on a piece of unlined paper, assess the way in which they have been placed in terms of the left-hand and right-hand sides of the page. When numbers occupy space more to the left of the page, the writer is always mindful of security. They tend to accumulate possessions and are always aware of their own material safety and standing. When placed towards the right side of the page, the writer wants to forget the past; the future offers more opportunity in this writer's mind.

Base lines

As in normal handwriting, consider the base line of the writing. When the line slants upward, the writer will exhibit optimism; should the line slope downward, they will be more pessimistic. A straight base line suggests someone who gets things done, is practical and tends to set and achieve their goals. The more consistent the base line, the more this will be so.

When a number falls below the base line, some carelessness with material matters will be present. The way in which the number is actually created will help here.

There is only one number that may be 'allowed' to extend below the base line and that is the number 9. As a rule, the 9 is started on the right, comes to the left in a loop and is then finished in a straight downstroke. Often, this extends below the base line and this is a very common practice. However, the 9 may be written like an upside-down number 6. This is an indication that the writer dislikes taking precipitate action – indeed, they may try to avoid initiating action altogether in some cases. This will be accentuated if the number is written in a reverse action, started at the bottom and completed at the top of the 9.

Form and pressure

Individual numbers should be examined for the way they are formed and placed in relation to the others. Most often, the number 1 is the first to be written, unless it is part of a calculation. As everything else that follows should line up with this first stroke, how the number is made and where it is placed takes on extra importance. Check the pressure used, note if it is a straightforward downstroke with no embellishments, or whether it has curves or other variations. A small tick at the top or base, for example, reflects impatience or a temper.

Slant

Compare the slant of the number with the handwriting. If it has the same inclination, the writer is content with their situation in life. A figure that reclines to the left when the writing also inclines to the left means a person who is guarded where money and possessions are concerned. Should the number incline and the writing recline, the writer is likely to be a little careless and unable to keep to a budget; this is someone who is easily tempted to overspend.

Columns

Columns of figures should be compiled in a straight line, one figure under another all the way down. This will indicate a fairly decisive nature, someone well able to cope with all of life's little problems.

A wavy line suggests a more indecisive type, someone apt to waver and have difficulties exhibiting self-confidence. If the column veers to the right the writer will display increasing confidence as the work progresses. They will be more inclined to risk the odd chance here and there. If the column reclines to the left of the page, the writer will be slightly introverted and not so prepared to take risks of any kind.

When all the numbers are smoothly written, it shows a sober and serious attitude toward material matters. If small and precisely made, there may be routine involvement in, or concentration on, financial matters. This often shows in the handwriting of accountants or other people who deal directly with cash.

Alterations

When numbers are indistinctly written, there will be a negligent attitude to all material things. Should a number be touched up or altered, the writer probably has a slightly neurotic approach, an anxiety with financial matters and attendant problems. Decorative numbers denotes a daydreamer who tends to stay away from the reality of monetary affairs. Clumsily written numbers are a suggestion of being poor at maths and imply neglect of practical concerns.

Chapter 18

PUNCTUATION

Punctuation is vital to communication. As a rule, most educated writers pay fairly strict attention to the way they make and place their punctuation marks. Generally, such a writer will plan a careful path through the message to ensure not only that what they write will be readable but also that the message will be clearly understood. They will be aware that a change in the punctuation can change the meaning of the written matter.

Unfortunately, many people simply do not know how to use punctuation marks correctly, and you should bear this in mind during your analysis and compare your conclusions here with those in other sections.

The use of punctuation in a piece of writing can show you both the mood of the writer at the time and their overall concern about precision and attention to detail.

Perhaps one of the best ways to assess this feature of handwriting analysis is to read the message aloud to yourself exactly the way it has been written. It is very important that you read exactly what is there and not what you *think* is there or *should be* there. This is by far the most accurate way of assessing the punctuation as, when done carefully, it ensures that you are accurately considering the punctuation the writer has placed and not imposing your own style on the assessment.

Writing style

Assess the style of the writing first. Different writers will tend to have a fairly consistent style of punctuation. Someone writing in a formal style will tend to follow the grammatical rules of punctuation fairly strictly. On the other hand, someone with a freer style may use less punctuation and be looser in their application. In either case, the marks must be appropriate to the overall style and must ensure that the message they are trying to communicate comes over perfectly clearly.

In general, the greater the precision with which punctuation marks are used, the more precise and controlled the writer.

The correct placing of a punctuation mark indicates attention to detail, provided it is perfectly positioned in line with the base of the letter immediately preceding it. This is an indication of a good emotional and intellectual balance at the time of writing. A writer who meticulously dots every i or crosses every t with care and precision (dealt with in Chapters 15 and 16) is likely also to have good punctuation and is showing that they are able to follow the correct procedure in such matters and that those procedures matter to them.

In a free-flowing and well-written script, poor punctuation usually means that the writer is not interested in the details but is more concerned with getting their message across. They are more likely to be hasty and imaginative, concerned with the overall picture rather than the minutiae of detail.

Maintaining consistency

Often, writers start well but take less care as they carry on. They become more concerned with what they are writing than how they write. This does not lessen their abilities in any way – in fact, it is perfectly normal and something which happens when most of us write, so you should expect the use of punctuation to become less precise as you work through a piece of writing. If this is not the case, it underlines the importance of precision in the writer's personality.

One excellent method of detecting a mood change in any sample of handwriting is to study the position of the punctuation very carefully. If it is positioned well at the start of the letter but becomes quite markedly different towards the end, it is firm evidence that the writer has become careless and the earlier control has gone. This can indicate that control does not come naturally to them, but they have to make a conscious effort to achieve it.

Do make a thorough examination of the envelope in which that letter was enclosed, as this can often give extra clues to the mood of the writer at the time of writing. A careful analysis of the envelope is dealt with more fully in chapter 19.

Position of marks

If the punctuation marks are higher than the base line, this indicates that the writer was in quite a cheerful frame of mind while writing, especially so if the base line of the script also rises. Conversely, punctuation marks placed below the line suggest some moodiness or perhaps even depression – the writer was perhaps feeling generally unhappy, or possibly they were uncomfortable with the message they had to convey in the letter.

Over-punctuated and under-punctuated work

When a handwriting sample seems to be overrun with dots, colons, semi-colons, full stops or other punctuation marks, however, the writer is rather obsessed with unnecessary detail.

Excessive punctuation shows a worrier; someone who must impress and is inclined to exaggeration, the type that finds it difficult to let go of a problem long after it has ceased to have any importance or even remain of concern. Often, this writer tends to underline words and phrases or other parts of the letter in an effort to create extra meaning.

An example of excessive punctuation

centre available   Contact your
operator for details When you
an SMS message from your phone
works message centre tries to
the message to the receiving phone
hone numbers are erased without
You cannot undo this

An example of no punctuation

When a letter is written with a lack of punctuation marks it shows the writer was not thinking straight at the time. It also indicates some selfishness, someone who cannot be bothered with details, a rebel perhaps or just the stubborn type who likes to be, or feels they must be, different.

A colon or a full stop after a signature is a strong indication of a writer who must have the last word.

Chapter 19

ENVELOPES

Some handwriting analysts are inclined to forget the envelope in their overall assessment. In their defence, some say that the envelope may reveal an artificial style of writing because of what it is. The rules governing the size and proportions of envelopes and the way they are addressed are fairly rigid. Other analysts feel it is of prime importance, curiously enough for nearly all the same reasons.

An envelope is a specially constructed case for a letter. It may be small or quite large; it may be cheap or high quality and – very important – it can be of any colour. Each of these factors will help you make an additional analysis of the character and personality of the person who wrote it. Where a person positions the address on an envelope and also how they write that address reveals a lot about their personality; both are important in interpretation.

Legibility

You will expect the name and address to be legible, for not only must the postman be able to read it, the writer also needs to make a good impression on the addressee. This is yet another way in which the writer subconsciously tells the reader how they wish to be viewed, for the way they write on an envelope is regarded as being their 'public' face. The 'private' face is on the letter inside.

If the address is illegible, this implies a 'don't care' attitude, a writer who is careless, selfish and too rude to think about the effect of an illegible script on the envelope; other people's opinions or problems don't matter. It may also be the sign of a rebel.

Comparison with the letter

When the writing on an envelope is the same as the writing on the letter inside, it shows the writer is just what they seem to be: no airs and graces here. If the handwriting is larger on the envelope than on the letter, the writer is trying to impress the recipient or boost their own ego. If it is smaller than the writing inside, it may be displaying false modesty or, perhaps, the writer is much more confident than they might wish to appear.

Large and small writing

Large writing on an envelope is the sign of an extrovert with an expressive personality who has to be at the centre of attention at all times. Very much a 'me first, women and children next' attitude.

If the writing is very small, the head will rule the heart and mental pursuits will attract the writer far more than physical activities. The writing suggests that the person is modest but can very often also indicate a rather calculating personality.

An address written in a small and cramped hand indicates repression with a fear of getting involved. Such a writer tends to bottle up their feelings instead of expressing them.

The placement of the address

The envelope is divided into four quarters and the quarter in which the writer places the address is the first thing to consider. The quickest way to mark the quarters so that you can make your assessment is to fold the envelope in half, first vertically and then horizontally, then flatten it out.

Ideally, the address should start halfway down the envelope and be written centrally. This illustrates a knowledge of the correct etiquette, and the writer's good balance and judgement.

An address placed too high indicates a careless person, perhaps a dreamer who is lacking in self-confidence. If the address is placed too low, this is a sign of a pessimist and someone for whom material things are particularly important.

If the address is predominantly in the top left quarter of the envelope, it suggests the writer is more of a daydreamer rather than a doer, although they are likely to have an enquiring mind, and this can mean that they are liable to miss out on opportunities in life. They also tend to be emotional and easily moved.

An address in the bottom left quarter indicates the money-minded and materialistic type. The writer will often neglect emotional needs in favour of job or career considerations. They may be a collector or just plain acquisitive.

When the address is placed in the top right quarter, it suggests that the writer has an impulsive, warm and affectionate nature. They will like to take the initiative and can be emotionally demonstrative and affectionate.

Placing the address in the bottom right quarter implies a writer with a love of adventure. While they are realistic, down-to-earth, even slightly cynical with few illusions, they do take the occasional chance if and when the opportunity arises.

The address made in the traditionally stepped indented formation from the top left to the bottom right denotes a slightly unsure, cautious type who should not be hurried into making decisions. If they can not only remember but also continue to observe what they were taught while they were still at school, it is obvious that this is not the writing of a leader, whatever the actual script may imply. This is one of the reasons why the age of the writer should be known. Older people are more likely to follow convention than the young because of their less questioning attitude towards education, so in an older person's writing this may simply indicate that they are precise and tend to follow the rules they have learned.

Encircled capitals and unusual features

An address written with encircled capital letters shows a self-protective style of writing and acts as a warning. Basically, it is a 'keep-off' sign. The writer really wants to be left alone and has an urgent need to feel secure at all times.

Underlining may well stress the importance of the letter but it also reveals that far too much of the writer's time is wasted on unnecessary trivia and they are likely to neglect realities. This is especially so when all the words are emphasised with underlining.

Unusually shaped letters in an address imply an original mind, but the more ostentation the writer employs, the more likely it is that it will be accompanied by bad taste. It is also possible that the writer has artistic inclinations.

Slant

A writer with left-slanted script on the envelope is withdrawn, prefers to keep the world at bay, may not be a good mixer and may not even like company. It is rather difficult to get these people out of their shell.

Right-slanted script indicates a sociable, open and easygoing nature, one who is usually friendly and reasonable at all times. Should the script be over-inclined to the right, expect to find an enthusiast who may not always take in details.

Writing in an upright hand indicates a person who is largely independent and is more than able to make decisions and act on them. This is a sign of the self-sufficient type who knows what is expected of them but may not necessarily go along with the herd.

Chapter 20

INK AND PAPER COLOURS

The role of colour in the way we dress, behave, or even how we purchase goods is so much part of our culture that it is even embedded in the language. We talk of black moods or feeling blue, of being green with envy or under the influence of the green-eyed monster, jealousy. Yellow is linked with cowardice, red with passion or rage, white with temper. We know about warm and cold colours, the soothing effects of some tones and colour combinations and the harsh effects of others. There is no escaping the association of colour, mood and personality.

It is now accepted that the dark colours are associated with the passive responses in our temperament. They equate with the dark, a time of rest, lowered resistance and a general slowing-down. Lighter and brighter colours, on the other hand, are associated with daylight and suggest activity, incentive and energy. You can see this quite clearly in the colours people choose for clothes. People linked with activity and energy tend to wear lighter, stronger, 'active' colours, especially in informal situations. People who are more restrained and responsible – perhaps even a little dull – wear darker, 'passive' colours. This is particularly true in a serious business environment.

This means, of course, that the colours we choose to wear are giving messages to those around us by reflecting our mood and inner desires of that day – at the start of it at least. They are a way of expressing individual moods – and can be used by others to assess those mood changes. You only need to consider how carefully you might select the colour and style of your clothes for a job interview or an important meeting, for example, to understand that this is true. Similarly, if you are going to meet your partner, in whatever stage of a relationship, what you wear suggests what you may be expecting of them.

In our surroundings too, colour has important effects on our mood and the colours we choose for interior decor, for example, should be in keeping with our own responses and the use to which the room will be put. Stark red and black might not be the best choice for a room in which you want to relax and wind down after a hard day at work, for example.

Psychologists have studied mood changes for years and are now actively using colour to understand more about people; some of their observations are remarkably accurate and very perceptive. They can also use colour in therapy to influence the way we think and feel.

There are all kinds of subtleties associated with colour, but most people agree on some basic areas of association. These are, however, sometimes associated with culture, so exercise a note of caution when thinking about a particular use of colour. For example, white is the traditional wedding colour in the UK and USA, but in India the wedding colour is red. In the West, black is the colour of mourning, but in the Far East, white has that traditional association.

For the most part, however, red is said to be passionate, while pink is the true romantic's colour. Blue is intense and deep. White is traditionally the colour of purity. Green is said to be receptive, brown is materialistic and earthy. Yellow is linked with the mentally active and black is sexy or secretive.

Ink and paper colours

The same principles can be applied to handwriting analysis. The colour of paper and ink, provided it is used consistently by a writer rather than on one particular occasion, has a definite bearing on their personality and inner feelings.

Most young people pass through many experimental phases before they finally settle down and consistently use a particular colour. They are liable to change to a different fashion overnight every night in some cases and they can easily adopt an ink colour that will show this for what it is – a passing phase. However, their permanent choice is a free one and will reflect their behaviour patterns.

Remember that when writers do use an unusual colour, you may have to put it down to well-meaning but misguided friends who give stationery that the writer would not have chosen for themselves! So, if you have a sample of writing in pink ink on a brown paper come before you, it would be wise to make sure it is the writer's preferred choice before you draw any alarming conclusions.

While the range of paper colours is vast, most people will use varying shades of white or cream. Occasionally, a writer will prefer to be different, and if they choose an unusual colour on a regular basis, then it is relevant to your handwriting assessment. The significance of the choice of colour is largely the same for paper and ink, as detailed below.

Blue

The vast majority of writers are inclined to use blue ink, most often light blue. Blue suggests an outgoing, warm and sympathetic personality. Royal blue is used largely by those who like to care for others: nurses or teachers. Blue is often used by editors, and it is from the use of a blue pen to correct author's mistakes on a manuscript that we get the term 'blue pencil'.

Green

Green ink is more likely to be used by immature characters, the young and impressionable of either sex. Such a writer may be an exhibitionist or an individualist who cannot bear to be one of the crowd and has to be seen to be different. These people have to impress, to be the centre of attention, but usually all they seem to do is show off their inexperience and immaturity. However, in their favour is the fact that many who use this colour are highly creative and artistic.

Brown

Those who regularly use brown ink like to be noticed but refrain from actively pushing themselves to the forefront. One of their prime concerns is personal security; they do not like to take chances.

Black

Black ink is used by those who need to be clearly understood at all times; they allow little margin for error. Such writers are often intolerant and do not suffer fools gladly under any circumstances. Ambition and personal prestige matter – all the time. Their outlook may tend towards the formal, certainly in the work place, and they may well be involved in work that requires precision or calculation.

Red

Red ink, when used regularly, suggests that the writer must be noticed. These people feel they are different and like to shock those around them. They are quite active, restless and full of excitement and seem to live on their nerves. Writers like this have to experience everything at first hand. As leaders, it is rare for them to ask others to do things they themselves cannot do; they prefer always to lead by example.

Violet

Violet ink is also often used by those who wish to impress but for quite different reasons. They are social butterflies, female and male. The ladies are known for their grace and elegance, whatever age they may be. Men who regularly use this colour tend to be effeminate, weak-willed and submissive. Often, the past may hold more than the future for these people.

Gold and silver

Those who use yellow or gold ink are often naturally artistic and may be intuitive. As a rule, they are not very practical. Silver or grey ink suggests a detached view of life, and this writer will want as much independence as they can get.

Chapter 21

LOOPS: EMOTIONAL
AND SEXUAL POINTERS

L oops in handwriting always show emotion, the quality and
level of which are indicated by the pressure used, and the size
and construction of the loops. Sexual drive is shown in
handwriting by the formation of the lower case letters g and y and,
to a slightly lesser extent, the lower case letters f and j, particularly
if made with a triangular loop (see page 127). The capital letter J
can also show some indications of sexual drive (see page 162). The
descenders, or lower loops, of these letters reveal subconscious
instincts, sexual preferences, inclinations and sexual drives.

To understand these strokes it is necessary to study many
samples of handwriting in some depth. Never take just one example
of a single g or y in isolation as proof of a feature of someone's
personality. Also, even though some handwriting traits may be
indicative of some unusual sexual proclivity, it does not mean that
the writer either practises or is even aware of it. It may indicate
simply a latent tendency or an aspect of their overall emotional
nature. For example, some men may have a strong feminine side
that makes them particularly caring individuals but has no other
sexual significance.

Our emotions are among the most closely guarded areas of our
lives and most people find it hard – most particularly in times of
stress – to be totally honest with themselves, let alone with another
person, however close they may be. This self-control, which we
exercise to a greater or lesser degree all the time, is revealed by the
way we write and it is important for potential graphologists to
remember this when considering an analysis.

When a loop to the g or y is being formed, the impulse is to let the pen go downwards to form the stem and then finish the letter by bringing the pen smoothly upward and over to form a loop. In order to make the pen travel downwards, the writer has to make a conscious muscle movement of the hand to control the changing direction. When this motion is relaxed, the stroke is automatically rounded and flows evenly. When there is stress or tension, this rhythm is disturbed, making any movements of the pen unco-ordinated and producing loops that will vary in shape, size and formation.

The crossing of the downstroke by the upstroke is particularly significant, but take into account that the left slant tends to imply introspection while the right slant indicates extroversion and sociability.

Pressure

The sensuality of the writer can be assessed from the amount of pressure used when the writer creates the lower zone strokes and loops. Heavy pressure suggests a sensuous personality, light pressure generally suggests a lower libido, and varying pressure generally implies that something is not quite right when it comes to the sexual or emotional life of the writer. This is because the pressure shows the writer's energy and vitality – stronger pressure for greater energy and sensuality.

Height and shape of loops

The height and depth of the letters' upper or lower extensions also give insights into emotional matters, longer strokes indicating a more active sexual life. The rounder or softer the loops appear, the more the writer's nature will be soft and yielding.

As the fullness of the loop expresses depth of feeling and imagination, the larger the loop, the more emotional and vivid the writer's imagination will be. The longer the downstroke, the more energy is shown in their personality. This also reveals the depth of their instinctive physical drives.

A more angular construction denotes a more aggressive character, even to the point where hard, spiky downstrokes can indicate a streak of mental or physical cruelty. Pointed loops nearly always mean the writer has a rebel streak, the development of which is determined by the sharpness of the point. Impotence or lack of interest is implied by poorly made or short, light strokes into the lower zone.

Normal and regular loops

Lower loops that go straight down, move smoothly to the left, rise and cross back over the original line are considered 'normal' in handwriting analysis. A normal emotional and sexual approach is seen in well-rounded loops, generously long and crossed at the bottom of the stem. The stroke goes straight down and then crosses over to the right.

This kind of loop shows warmth of emotion, healthy physical desire and an ability to give and receive love and affection.

Monotonous, regular loops like the following sample indicate a dull temperament with little imagination or sensitivity. These little loops also show repression of emotional and sexual urges with some resulting tension.

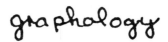

Slanting loops

The way the loops of the g and y slant in their lower development – left, right, or straight down – is significant. The g and the y should be studied, when possible, within a word rather than when they fall at the end of the word, and throughout the sample.

If the loop slants to the left, it is an indication of negative past emotional experiences which influence the writer's emotions. This may often be an exceptionally strong tie to their mother. The instinct of this writer is to be introverted and withdrawn.

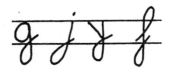

When the slant is to the right, it indicates a strongly influential father.

A right-slanted script with left-pointing descenders that are hook-like or arched suggest an avoidance of responsibility in the writer's emotional life. As in many other cases, problems of this kind are often the result of difficult experiences in the past which have not been resolved.

Left-sweeping loops

Small g and y descenders that sweep strongly to the left can have a variety of interpretations so it is important to consider the whole picture and not to draw conclusions from just one aspect of the handwriting.

The aspect of writing style is expressed by the long or inflated loop that is pushed to the left, or by strokes that shift to the left with a horizontal bias. This may also be seen when the capital J is written.

The first indication of this style of loop is one of emotional immaturity or sensitivity. This may be a very young person or someone who is over-sensitive to personal and sexual matters.

Wide, large loops that swing to the left, as in the following sample, are often seen in the script of young girls and are an expression of their emotional immaturity and impressionablity. This loop also shows a writer who could be in love with love, or who has an incomplete sex life.

This style can also indicate what is known in modern graphology as the Oedipus complex, or a strong attachment to the mother figure. It is therefore sometimes found in the writing of homosexuals, male or female. The loop may be wide and rounded and finish with a left-sweeping movement.

Alternatively, it may loop back on itself, as in the following example.

In a woman's handwriting, the strong lower loop swinging to the left is sometimes considered a symbol of the male organ and an indication of lesbian tendencies.

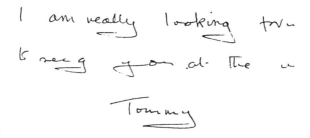

When the pull to the left is particularly strongly marked, in the writing of a man or woman, it is also a sign of introspection; the libido is turned inward and there is likely to be a considerable degree of narcissism.

Rounded and curled loops

Clear, rounded loops show a considerate, thoughtful and co-operative partner. They also reveal someone with imagination and a fairly emotional attitude to life, and the pressure will show the amount of sensuality and energy present – or the lack of it, according to the thickness of the strokes.

A rounded, figure 8-type of the letter g or y usually appears in the handwriting of people who have a strong desire for peace, harmony and emotional security and stability in domestic life. It can appear in the writing of a woman who wants a child but may be unable to do so for a variety of reasons, or in the writing of a man with a strong feminine, caring side.

The figure 8-type y or g can also, therefore, often appear in the handwriting of homosexuals, either male or female. It is not always possible to state categorically from this stroke if the writer is active or passive. However, when such descenders are long and made with quite a heavy pressure there is always a strong depth of feeling.

Lord o bomb the Germans
their women for thy sake,
if that is not so easy,
will pardon thy mistake.

Extremely strong desires are shown in this twisted form of the figure 8 in the writing of a female homosexual. The pointed base indicates aggression, while the heavy pressure shows plenty of energy and vitality. A strong streak of materialism is also shown.

When the descenders are curled or rolled-up, any interest in sexual matters is likely to be unusual, even abnormal in some cases. People who write like this are not always honest with themselves or others and they can have quite eccentric ideas about sex.

Occasionally the lower loop may be made in the shape of a double loop – a distorted figure 8 – and is frequently found in the writing of people who have literary talent.

Lord o bomb the Germans
their women for thy sake,
if that is not so easy,
will pardon thy mistake..

Large and long loops

Large, inflated loops can indicate active sexual fantasies. The huge loops in the handwriting below are a sign of a vivid emotional and sexual imagination and an inflated ego, which may be compensating for a well-hidden inferiority complex. These writers indulge in sexual fantasy to make up for their lack of a sense of reality. They can be boastful, theatrical in manner and show a need to attract attention and admiration.

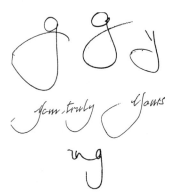

Long, heavy loops written with heavy pressure are a sign of outdoor activity – the sporting individual, athlete or person interested in physical fitness. They are also likely to be realistic and practical. This shows warm-heartedness and affection toward those close to them.

Long loops with heavy pressure and a smudged or blurred appearance show strong sexual impulses with demanding and sensual appetites. There is an animal or earthy approach to love and sex, and in extreme cases the writer may even be coarse and vulgar.

Long, narrow loops indicate tension and frustration. The writer may have trouble in coping with their feelings and might be unable to sustain relationships. When the loops are pointed, it is a sure sign of a bad temper.

Varying loops

Handwriting of an even rhythm indicates inner harmony and balance that can withstand strong external pressure, whereas handwriting that is unrhythmic and uneven shows an excitable and emotionally neurotic personality which lacks that inner balance. When the descenders of the g and y are extremely odd, eccentric or even bizarre, they imply nervous disorders, inhibitions, tension, sexual and physical disturbances or illness, and aggressiveness. In extreme cases, they may also indicate a degree of sadism, masochism, excessive sexual fantasies or homosexuality.

It is important to establish first whether weak or trembling strokes are a sign of physical illness or disability, old age or even nervous exhaustion. It would be misleading to attribute emotional interpretations to handwriting characteristics which result purely from physical symptoms. When the downstrokes are light and trembling, such as that seen in the handwriting of this senile writer, thoughts rarely lead to action.

Since the formation of loops reflect emotional and sexual preferences, it is logical that variations from what is considered the accepted pattern can imply some movement away from the norm. You will recall that the natural movement when writing g or y is a downward stroke followed by an upward swing. When a writer deviates from this procedure, either by cutting off a crossing stroke, changing direction, interrupting the motion or abruptly ending a stroke without a crossing, they are subconsciously controlling the natural action. Such alterations reveal inhibition, repression, a sexual quirk or even a deficiency.

When loops vary in shape and size, the writer has a changeable and inconsistent nature. They will be restless, moody and could even be emotionally unstable at times.

Lazy Red Dog.

I remember you long
of all everyone wants
sex — always a fair

Narrow or thin strokes are an indication of a repressed or inhibited emotional and sexual desire, perhaps caused by negative past experiences.

Any loop that is broken at the bottom is a sign of hidden fears and apprehension about sexual matters. This writer is likely to be conventionally correct and has a strictly correct code of sexual behaviour.

g

An unfinished loop written in the style of the sample below is a sign of frigidity or impotence. If the stroke looks weak the writer may be ill.

writing

Small loops that do not cross the stem shows emotional and sexual anxiety. Handwriting with a varying slant, as shown here, is a sign of irritability, and emotional inconsistency.

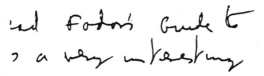

Unlooped and missing downstrokes

A straight line downward, used instead of a loop, shows a writer who may sublimate emotional and sexual desire into other activities, using the energy in business, home or other interests. These writers often show good judgement but they are also likely to have a fatalistic attitude to life. Once again, when a stroke is weak-looking, the cause may be a health matter.

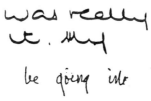

This rather heavy, unlooped downstroke, thickening at the bottom of the stem, shows that the writer has a hot temper. Someone who makes their downstrokes in this way can be deceitful emotionally and sexually. Although they may claim to be sexually sensitive, this is not the case and they can be quite aggressive in their attitude.

The following script indicates controlled aggression. The writer is probably obsessive and exercises so much control of their emotions that no one can get close to them, although the small loop at the base of the letter g suggests the writer longs for more material security.

Narrow downward strokes without a loop but with tiny hooks suggest impotence and frigidity. If there is a loop it will be poorly made with very light pressure.

Lower extensions that curl under, or are absent, show inadequacy and a stifling of the instinctive sex drive. There may be various reasons, one being fear of the sex act itself.

quickly

When handwriting is wholly in the middle zone with little or no attempt to make downstrokes, the writer may hide their emotional needs by concentrating their energies on other areas of their life. Their house may be beautiful, but it will not be a home.

handwriting again

Sincerely

Small loops

A very small loop at the end of the descender indicates a loner, one who prefers their own company. Their emotional and sexual life, if any, may be lacking in warmth and trust.

my

A narrow downward stroke that turns upward but does not cross the stem to complete the loop indicates emotional and sexual anxiety. The writer's nature tends to be somewhat irritable, probably because of frustration.

g   g

Short mini-curves to the left of the downstroke imply emotional and sexual immaturity, especially in young people. There may be a lack of constructive imagination.

anything

> anything

Heavy and exaggerated loops

The loop in the next sample has been made with heavy pressure and is slightly blurred in appearance. This implies rather strong physical appetites and desires.

These exaggerated lower lengths have been written with very light pressure, always a sign of sensitivity. There is a very strong, active imagination. The writer stretches the truth a little and likes to show off or hog the limelight.

Triangular loops are frequently a sign of sexual frustration or incompatibility. The writer can be something of a tyrant in the home and may even be socially aggressive as a result of their disappointment with their partner.

Loops within loops show compulsive behaviour patterns bordering on the obsessive. There is a streak of stubborn possessiveness in this personality that can get out of hand. Sexual interests are often out of the ordinary – this writer may be a voyeur, for example, or someone who enjoys erotic films but may shy away from actual sexual experience. This loop should not be confused with the female homosexual sign of the figure 8 (see page 121).

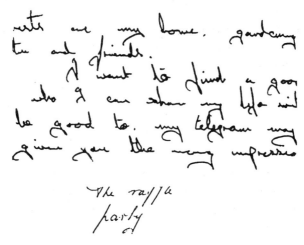

The grasping claw to the left (below) shows avoidance of responsibility, sexual or emotional, and also suggests a materialist. Someone who shows this feature in their handwriting often has a money complex. They will hoard and save furiously for a rainy day but, when that day comes, still not want to tap into their savings. Writers like this often have very strong family ties and may be clannish.

The long downstroke with a turned-up, angular stroke implies an aggressive nature and a stunted sexual desire, possibly through guilt feelings or emotional repression due to earlier negative experiences.

The swooping half-loops to the right formed by the next writer suggest a strong father image and are a sign of avarice, intolerance and a suspicious nature.

The writer is emotionally deceptive, unable or unwilling to trust others. They will also have quite a vivid imagination and be inclined to indulge in fantasies.

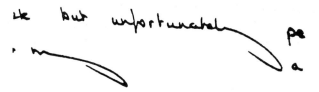

Spiky loops

Any pointed or spiky angles at the bottom of the downward stroke are a sign of repression, aggression and immaturity.

Short, spiky descenders that swing to the right from the base of the stem suggest the writer's sex drive is stifled or sublimated but the energies may be used in some form of altruistic work in the social area or other constructive outlet.

This unusual and angular formation distorts the lower loops and shows resentment and aggression. The writer may indulge in abnormal emotional or sexual behaviour. If the writer is a man, he is likely to have a strong feminine, caring side to his character.

These sickle-like strokes formed in half-open circles indicate a writer who is introverted, resentful and, possibly, emotionally obsessional.

Sexual symbols

Other sexual symbolism often appears in handwriting. Generally, this shows a preoccupation either with that part of the body, or abnormal sexual leanings involving the area.

Sexual symbols are most commonly found in the letters b, p and w. This is because parts of the body may be seen in these letters and therefore they tend to reflect the writer's tendencies and obsessions with them.

Emotional and sexual compatibility

Since handwriting reflects character and personality, it follows that if we compare our handwriting with that of others we should be able to improve our relationships by better understanding our own nature and that of our partners or colleagues. If the differences in handwriting between two or more people are carefully analysed over a period of time, that analysis can offer real insights into the personalities, emotions and needs of those people. This information can be used to create a greater degree of understanding and tolerance between them, thereby improving their relationships.

It is important always to remember, of course, that it is often not a good thing for a relationship if people are too similar – our differences make us unique and interesting to each other. However, if we have to work or live closely with other people for long periods, it is helpful for each person to have a greater insight into the nature of their friend, colleague or partner so that they can compensate for their own as well each other's character traits and make the relationship more smooth-running and successful.

Chapter 22

VOCATIONAL GUIDANCE

Y ou cannot use graphology to tell what a writer actually does for a living but you can use it to determine the career direction for which they appear most suited. This does not mean that they are not good at what they currently do, but someone looking for help with a career choice or considering a change of direction can gain some insight into what might be the best direction to take.

Career direction

Graphology is a most useful tool when advising the young as they start out, as it can highlight capabilities and aspects of their personality which will make them suited to one career or another. A full graphological analysis at a stage when a young person is making important choices in their studies or early work options can help them to make the most suitable choices and give them more chance of making a success of the line of study or the career they eventually select.

However, it is important to remember that, in the modern work environment, many people do not simply choose a career and stay in that niche all their lives. At different stages in their working lives, people can use graphology to analyse other potential options. It may help someone who is deciding whether a promotion which takes them in a different direction is, in fact, the right course for them. It may offer ideas to people who are dissatisfied with their current job and want a complete change of focus.

Of course, whenever the analysis is carried out, while it can help people find a comfortable niche which is both rewarding and fulfilling, it will not necessarily bring in more money.

Controlling stress at work

Another way in which graphology can help in the work environment is in assessing stress levels at work. It is an unfortunate fact that many people find their work stressful or are generally unhappy in their jobs for one reason or another, not necessarily associated with the workplace itself. The dissatisfaction could stem from domestic or personal difficulties, external stress, or tensions created within the work environment.

Unfortunately, far too many people keep their emotions on a tight rein and bottle up their real feelings, often for long periods at a time. This can be particularly evident if they feel either that the problem has nothing to do with their work and therefore they feel additional guilt that it may be affecting their performance, or when the problem is, perhaps, a difficult colleague or too much work-related pressure. In that case, the person may be afraid that they will lose their job if they cause problems for other members of staff. However, no one can keep the lid on stress indefinitely. If stress is not dealt with but is allowed to build up, the negative consequences will inevitably be increasingly harmful for everyone involved.

It would make sense, then, for human resources officers to maintain a study of the handwriting of all employees, whether in the confines of a small firm or as part of a larger group. As changes in the handwriting reveal mounting stress levels, problems may be addressed and hopefully resolved through direct action – counselling or other means – before crisis point is reached.

Co-worker compatibility

Irrespective of the type of work people are doing or the size of the group in which they work, it is essential that people who work together are able to get on well with each other. When employing staff, managers need to be very much aware of this so that when they select new employees or consider promotion or placement of existing staff, they can feel confident that the person they have chosen will fit well both into the job itself and also into the hierarchy of personalities existing in that department.

Having a graphological record of their staff and analysing the handwriting of potential employees can make this task an easier one. Even if only the most basic graphological principles are applied – as outlined below – the decision-maker can gain additional insight into the person they are interviewing. Obviously a more in-depth analysis will be even more revealing.

Analysis of the handwriting of an applicant for a senior management position is just as important as one for the youngster coming in to make the tea. If a business is run to optimum efficiency, it will be staffed by people who care for each other as well as for their work. If this is not the case in your organisation, you could be spending too much time fighting each other instead of the competition.

Inclined writing

The more handwriting slants to the right, the more emotionally responsive the writer is likely to be. Any trigger will result in a rapid response from these individuals. Those who write in this way are best suited to ever-changing conditions. They thrive on the stimulus of change and novelty. They respond to atmosphere – both good and bad, unfortunately – but they do not stay down for long; they bounce back quickly after set-backs, although a strong forward slant will indicate that they make take longer than others to get back on an even keel. They have a flair for taking most things in their stride, however, as they have an inbuilt resilience.

> I am a female aged
> and never before have
> my handwriting and
> Thanking you in antic

Anything that requires too much detailed work like record-keeping turns them off so, while they are among the most natural salesmen of this world, actually selling for a living is not really their forte as it involves too much detail. They are at their best when selling themselves, however, and they relate well to other people and like working with them. This is not the sign of a lone worker but of someone who should be working closely with other people.

Upright writing

When handwriting appears more or less upright, within four or five degrees from the vertical, the writer has a far more objective view of life. This writer rarely acts on impulse. They are more inclined to stand back and assess a problem from all angles before deciding on a course of action. Everything will be carefully considered so that they are sure that whatever they decide to do will achieve the desired result for the benefit of all concerned.

Although forthright and perfectly able to speak their mind, the upright writer rarely does so before carefully considering all the options. They may be judged by others to be cold-blooded, unfeeling or hard-hearted because of their degree of control and poise, for it is very rare for this writer to lose control in public. When it comes to business decisions, there is a certain amount of truth in this, as they are likely to be quite dispassionate when necessary. Decisions will be based only on the facts and figures, not on personal feelings, and consideration of 'the human factor' will not be high on the agenda.

In emotional partnerships, therefore, the other half has to be understanding and more responsive than most. If the delicate balance between them is to continue, the art of compromise must be very strongly developed.

Please could you send me
Birth Chart for the be

These people make good, if firm, leaders and decision-makers. They are not ideally suited to the caring professions, but will thrive in a hard-headed business environment.

Reclined writing

Writing that slopes backwards denotes a writer demonstrating that they find it difficult to trust others. They tend to pull away from people, from life, and even their obligations in some cases. Such a writer fears failure and hates to make mistakes. This may be because they feel, subconsciously, that they have been punished in some way for previous mistakes and are determined that this should never occur again. Such introverted thinking can become ingrained and is difficult to overcome. Experienced counselling or an exceptionally gifted partner can help some people to overcome these feelings but for many, this attitude stays with them throughout life.

Occasionally, a lack of trust in others can be the result of a specific emotional disturbance – a break-up with a long-term partner, perhaps or an experience of having been deceived by someone placed in a position of trust. This underlines the importance, where possible, of assessing more than one sample of handwriting.

> I hope you don't mind havin
> seperate reports in one envelope
> I have enclosed an extra stamp
> postage, and apologise for any

These people tend to work best in circumstances where they can make a positive difference by their controlled attitude and attention to detail. They make good 'backroom boys', the background workers who keep things running by their persistent effort.

Other relevant pointers

The smaller a person's handwriting, the more likely they are to be able to concentrate for long periods at a time. Those with large writing will find concentration more difficult and need constant change and variety.

When little loops appear in the stem of the letters d and t, the writer will be sensitive to criticism but will thrive on any form of personal appreciation. A word of thanks will give them all the encouragement they need, while an ill-considered rebuke will be more than usually hurtful.

This chapter has highlighted just a few of the areas to consider. Obviously a full analysis, working through the chapters in this book, will give a much better overview of personality and potential.

Chapter 23

DOODLES

A doodle is an unconsciously created graphic design made as the writer's mind concentrates on other things. It is as though the mind switches off, goes into neutral, and the body's reflexes automatically take over. As the doodle is regarded by some as a physical manifestation of repressed emotions and the thoughts of the person who created it, it is often used to assess character and personality.

Strictly speaking, a doodle is not writing but drawing, although the image may comprise letters, a word or words or even names. As a rule, however, it is just a collection of lines. The design can take many forms and be entirely abstract with dots or geometrical patterns, or be representational and depict animals or other objects; in fact, it can contain just about anything.

Each picture has a meaning behind it which can provide a key to what the writer really thinks of the person or situation with which they are faced or are likely to be faced in the near future. Occasionally, the person may be dwelling on past issues.

As a rule, a doodle is a repetitive action, for most people have their own favourite way of expressing their innermost thoughts. In fact, a repeated design is often the writer's way of easing a temporary problem, for it helps take the mind off whatever may be bothering them at the time. Most people feel the need to do something with their hands while pondering the possible ways of resolving a matter in hand.

Both the image itself and its position on the page, the colour used and the pressure of the pen on the paper are all relevant, so it is important to consider all the aspects before starting to draw any conclusions.

Non-doodlers

There are a few people, very few, who never doodle and these people are controlled, direct, precise and to the point. There is never any doubt what they mean or want. You know exactly where you stand with this type. They make excellent leaders but rarely show their feelings when they make a decision and act upon it. Something has to be done – and they make sure it is. They tend to stand by their decisions and not to dwell on them unnecessarily.

Doodles as symbols

A doodle is frequently a symbol of what is going on in the writer's mind at the time. The scope of this book is not broad enough to include a comprehensive list of all possible symbolic doodles, but hopefully the following examples will be useful in helping you consider a number of possibilities.

A non-aggressive doodler is one who creates rounded designs with curved lines, whereas someone with a more aggressive personality will create a drawing with many hard, spiky lines with arrows or other features suggestive of a hard nature.

Sometimes the motivation for a particular doodle is obvious. For example, when a design is all hearts and flowers, romance is probably at the root of the person's thinking. Circles, hearts and flowers all have sexual connotations as well but this is largely as a symbol of escapism – what the person might want rather than what they actually have. Circles are also a sign of independence.

Cloud formations, as shown at the top of the next page, refer to escapism but reveal deep-seated emotions when they are filled in, and an inability to cope.

Arrows, snakes and triangles are representative of sexual tension and its inherent problems. If anything is drawn in an angular style it suggests aggression or frustration and the pressure with which this is executed reveals the depth of the problem.

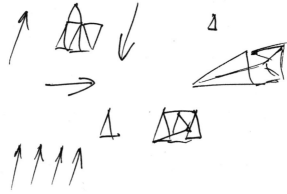

Faces and heads are symbolic of the writer's social nature, but the emphasis in the drawing can give more clues as to what they are thinking. When the eyes are emphasised, a heavy sexual content is implied, especially if there are also bushy eyebrows. Female eyes with long lashes suggest frustration.

In doodles, faces are either happy or sad, with the obvious implications on the mood of the doodler. If a doodle consists of a face or many faces looking to the left it shows reserve and some degree of introspection. A face drawn looking to the right suggests a more outgoing personality, a person who likes to be with people.

Self-portraiture is a sign of an inflated ego. Exaggerated drawings imply some kind of resentment. Head doodles are ego projections; the artist seeks approbation. A hat on the head is a sign of protection.

Houses symbolise security. The more detail in the drawing, the more idealistic the person's character, while the more elaborate the house, the more the writer wishes their needs would be fulfilled.

Lines and mazes are suggestive of inner conflict. Straight lines imply the no-nonsense type whose manner is too abrupt for some. The maze or web indicates frustration at a lack of achievement. Maze patterns are often created by those who cannot rather than will not solve the problem to hand.

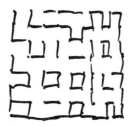

Many people draw a tree when occupied with their thoughts and the design of that tree reveals much about their inner nature. For example, a large number of leaves and branches would suggest a cerebral approach; the sturdier the base of the tree, the more physical the writer's approach to life will be.

Drawings of boats, cars and planes are symbols of a desire for the freedom to get away from it all. In moments of tension, doodling releases these feelings and can even ease the problem currently worrying the writer.

Symmetrical patterns show a good organising ability – the more complex the pattern, the stronger the person's power to get things done. If the patterns are partly shaded, this emphasises the administrative ability. If completely shaded, a strong sex drive is close to the surface.

Doodles that are heavily filled in suggest an anxiety complex. With heavy pressure and a poor or badly made shape, inner conflict could be raging within the doodler. Often, this signifies someone who is looking for the way out of a problem but is unable to find it without somebody getting hurt – including themselves.

Letters, words and figures

People also doodle with letters and words and this should be considered the domain of doodling, not strictly of graphology. Some people persistently scribble their name over and over again.

If a person doodles their own name repeatedly, it suggests a strong ego as this means they may be thinking of themselves a little too often. If they encircle the name, they may have an extra worry, perhaps of a temporary nature. The ring implies a form of self-defence through which enemies may not penetrate. A comparison of the normal signature with the doodled version often shows which way the person is thinking in terms of the problem to hand.

At times, people may write the name of whoever it is they are worrying about, or the name of the situation, problem or thing that has them temporarily in its grip.

Doodling any kind of a line above a name is symbolic of a need for protection. The writer may feel those in authority are about to impose discipline or a penalty for a past indiscretion. The line is a symbolic defence barrier to help prevent attack from above.

A paraph, or underscore, applied to a name or word has several different connotations, although all are variations on the theme of emphasis. A straight line is suggestive of thoroughness and finish; two small lines placed vertically across the line will emphasise this even more. Some authorities suggest this may also be a sign of money worries. A wavy line suggests a sense of humour, but an ostentatious squiggle implies poor taste and faulty judgement. A rising wavy line with two or three little wavy marks across it can suggest financial worries.

When figures feature in a doodle, it most often relates to current money problems. If the dollar, franc, mark, pound or any other money sign is woven within the fabric of the design and the colour yellow is used in part or in whole, this will be especially so.

Pen pressure

Most doodles are usually made with heavy pressure, which helps to indicate the level of worry. The heavier the pressure, the more concerned the writer is about the problem in hand. It can also indicate energy and even some aggressiveness in the character. Average or medium pressure suggests that the writer is not unduly worried by the problem to hand and indicates a need to keep the mind occupied rather than a focusing on a stressful situation. Light pressure can also indicate a sensitive nature. Changeable pressure shows moodiness or a fickle character, often influenced by the mood of the moment.

Position

Where the drawing is placed on a sheet of paper – that is, if it was empty to start with – is very important when assessing doodles. People often doodle in the margins of letters, official reports or even books. This always shows a very strong preoccupation with the problem. However, if a writer has started to doodle on a blank sheet of paper, then where it is placed can help the analyst decide not only on the type of personality but also the nature of the problem.

A doodle kept to the left-hand side of the page indicates past events are occupying the writer's thoughts. Someone or something may have a hold on them which is proving difficult to shake off and memories are very strong indeed.

If the doodle is on the right-hand side of the page, tomorrow is what matters most. The past has gone and the writer just cannot wait to move ahead. Attention to detail may not be a strong feature.

When the doodle is placed exactly in the middle of the empty page, the doodler wants and needs to be noticed. This writer will almost certainly have an extrovert personality. However, while little may be shown outwardly, there is almost always an inner desire for security.

A doodle at the top of the paper belongs to a writer with little time for formality. They tend to be over-enthusiastic and can forget where they are.

When placed at the bottom of the page, a doodle symbolises the follower rather than leader. The person is likely to lack initiative and may even exhibit a negative approach to life in general.

Ink colour

As I discussed in Chapter 20, the colour of ink regularly used by a writer has certain meanings and, for doodlers, these observations should help when you begin to assess them. Most avid doodlers do not mix colours as changing pens actually introduces a conscious action into what is a subconscious one. If they do, look at the dominant colour and make your assessment from there.

Blue is the most common colour used, usually light blue. When blue ink is used it suggests a normal and fairly well-balanced, outgoing personality.

When a series of different coloured inks are used in a doodle, then the different colours employed all add their meaning to the overall design.

When a doodle is drawn entirely in one ink colour other than blue, then that design will take on an extra meaning.

Green ink is used by the immature character, those of either sex who are easily impressed. These writers need to make their mark and be the centre of attention. There could be a tinge of envy or jealousy in their overall make-up. Green also suggests a creative and artistic nature.

Users of brown ink like to be noticed but are not especially pushy. As a rule they worry about their personal security and do not take chances. Basically, they have plenty of common sense.

Those who use black ink like to be clearly understood and they leave little margin for error; they can be quite intolerant at times and are inclined to be rather formal. If black is dominant in a doodle, the writer may be suffering from depression.

Those who doodle in red ink feel they are different from other people. They like to shock and are quite restless. The root cause could be sexual. Generally speaking, they are leaders rather than followers.

If violet ink is used in a doodle, expect to find someone who needs to impress; these people are inclined to be rather genteel, social butterflies, noted for their grace and elegance, but they are basically weak-willed, emotionally inconstant and inclined to be submissive.

Those who use yellow or gold ink are often naturally artistic and may be intuitive. There may be health or money worries, however.

Silver or grey ink suggest a detached view of life; these writers like their independence.

Chapter 24

THE SIGNATURE

The main body of handwriting in a letter is by far and away the best indication of the writer's emotional, mental and physical state at the time of writing – it reflects the inner person. The signature, on the other hand, reveals the way the writer wants to be seen by those around them – it shows the image they wish to present to the world.

Once we establish our handwriting style it becomes a part of us. We know it reflects our character and personality in the same way as how we smile, shake hands or walk. This is especially true of the signature. In our early years it is consciously formed as we are so self-aware, but as time goes by we become less so. Gradually, our subconscious takes over, guiding the actions of our hands and the pressure, speed and direction of our writing.

Our signature is obviously the thing we write most often. It is unique; no two signatures are identical, any more than there are two sets of identical fingerprints.

The signature, then, speaks to the graphologist in the same way as any other piece of writing, but it can reveal deeper psychological truths. This is because the signature stands for the writer themselves – it is their persona on paper. In general, it shows how they wish the world to see them; in detail it can also show characteristics they might want to hide.

A signature can therefore be the most difficult form of handwriting to analyse. It is a specialised area of graphology which demands close study because the signature of a person, more than anything else, is the symbol of the ego of the writer. Every single angle, curve, dot, letter and slant must be analysed in detail and then judged according to its relative importance in the whole word.

A signature remains basically the same once it is formed but it can and does vary with emotional disturbances, ill-health and, of course, old age. All these factors need to be taken into consideration when undertaking an analysis. It is therefore always helpful to have several specimens of a signature, if possible. As with any handwriting, the signature written when the person was relaxed and in good health is likely to differ from the one written when they were in pain or when unhappy. This highlights why it is important to be careful when making rash judgements based on a single signature. For a fuller analysis, a few lines of the writer's handwriting should accompany the signature. The best situation, and one in which you can make the most accurate analysis, is one in which you have several examples of both handwriting and signatures, all written at different times.

Even when a signature is illegible or abridged, it still retains the dominant characteristics and personality of the writer and gives clues to their individual identity. It still shows the writer both as they want to be seen and as they really are underneath.

When a signature is similarly written by several members of the same family, it is not necessarily a hereditary trait but it could arise because the individuals have similar characteristics or because they are copying the signature of a parent or some other relative they admire.

Dual signatures

People often employ two quite different signatures: one for their business or professional concerns, the other for more private and personal affairs. For this reason alone, one should exercise the greatest caution when assessing a single signature, especially if no further sample of handwriting is available for comparison. Two kinds of signature, in particular, lend themselves to misinterpretation: that of a newly married woman and the much-repeated signature of an official.

The woman who has just married and who may not like, or may not have grown used to, her new surname, surroundings, friends or relatives, can find it hard to adjust. She could feel she has lost her identity and may well write her first name larger than her new surname. Until the signature becomes unconscious and her natural style is absorbed, the signature will not be a good overall indication for the graphologist as it will primarily reflect her current unease.

When officials repeat their signature countless times every day, it becomes little more than a hieroglyph, distinctive as their mark perhaps, and difficult to forge, but virtually indecipherable for any other purpose. It is not the normal signature that person would use to a friend or relative, or even a close colleague. As the second of their two signatures, it reflects only their public and not their private image.

Position of the signature

Where the writer places their signature in relation to the rest of the script after they have finished the main body of the work has a great significance. People whose work involves receiving and sending a lot of letters tend to adopt the company style for both business and personal letters, even when the letters have nothing to do with work. Because of changes in business practice, therefore, there have also been changes in the way people sign both business and personal letters.

Signatures are normally found at the end of a letter, note or memo. It may be close to the last line or some distance away; it can be placed on the left-hand side of the page, in the centre or on the right-hand side of the paper. There has been a lot of discussion and dissension as to the 'correct' place for the writer to sign. In the past, it was always considered correct to sign a letter very slightly to the right of centre, at a visually comfortable distance from the last line. However, this was based on the traditional layout of a business letter in which the closing salutation – 'Yours sincerely', or whatever – was placed in the centre of the page.

Modern business letters are now almost always keyed on a computer and printed in a blocked style, so that the salutation is placed on the left-hand side. Modern letter-writing etiquette is also much more flexible than it once was, so it has become acceptable for a signature to appear almost anywhere at the end of a letter or document. There is no longer an accepted standard either generally or even within one company. For example, one multinational, London-based company actually has a space on the right-hand side of the top line of the first page for the writer to put their signature. The left-hand side is reserved for the name of the addressee. However, despite all these changes, the following observations and analyses on signature position still hold good for most people.

When the signature is placed very slightly to the right of centre and at a normal distance from the last line, the writer enjoys a good social life, is relatively outgoing, shows a good sense of initiative and is reasonably optimistic. If the signature is placed directly in the centre, these attributes are enhanced. Also, while the writer likes to be centre stage as much as possible, there will be just a hint of caution in their overall make-up.

When the signature is placed on the extreme right-hand side of the page, expect to find a lively, active character with a fair share of impatience and nervous energy.

Any signature written slightly to the left of the centre of the page suggests an inherently cautious or self-defensive, protective streak, according to how far to the left of the page the signature is sited.

When placed on the extreme left-hand side of the page, this generally indicates a lack of confidence in the writer, perhaps some kind of inner isolation and a withdrawn nature. A word of caution is necessary here, however, as the blocked business letter style mentioned above means that this is the most usual position for business people to sign letters. It is important to enquire, therefore, whether the writer is used to signing business letters on the left-hand side on a regular basis and if this is the case, then not too much store should be set by this aspect of the analysis. Refer to other traits in the signature or, preferably, in the handwriting itself, for a more accurate judgement.

The further the signature is placed away from the last line of the letter, the more the writer may be suggesting that they want little or nothing to with what is written – and what is written may not even be wholly truthful. When placed very close to the text, the writer is assuring the recipient of their honesty and belief in what they have just written and is happy to be associated with the contents of the letter.

Size of the signature

A signature written smaller than the text suggests introversion. The writer may be sensitive and mild. However, they may also be a schemer who deliberately sets out to give this impression in order to gain an advantage.

A signature written larger than the main body of text denotes the confident and forceful type, someone who moves smoothly through life. If the signature is quite considerably larger than the text, expect to find selfishness, overconfidence, pride and pretentiousness, with some expansiveness thrown in for good measure.

An over-large and exaggerated signature is always the sign of a strong ego but it can also be a compensation for inner feelings of inferiority. This should be supported by features found elsewhere in the person's handwriting.

General attributes of signatures

Bear in mind when looking at how a person writes their signature, that they may take a slightly different approach depending on the letter they are signing. The same person will use just their first name for a personal letter or a letter to a close colleague, their full name to a less well-known colleague and their initials and surname when writing to someone they do not know. All these points have a bearing on the interpretation you give.

A clear signature without embellishment indicates reliability and a fairly conservative approach to life – this indicates the natural type.

An illegible signature indicates carelessness, selfishness, bad manners and downright rudeness. The writer cares little for you, being interested only in what they have written.

When the first and family name look fairly well balanced, it shows inner harmony between the private and social life of the writer.

A signature with initials only followed by the name shows a writer who is likely to be rather formal. They will be cautious and conservative, the type who follows the rules without much spontaneity.

When a person writes their first and last names in full they may tend to be a little full of themselves. If they use all their first names with their surname, they may be pompous and a snob.

When the lower zone is exaggerated, expect to find a writer who is rather defensive with some feelings of inferiority. They are likely to be quite imaginative, but perhaps with a tendency towards materialism.

When dots appear anywhere in the signature, there will be a degree of inhibition in the writer's character. If a dot is placed after the signature, the writer is implying the matter is finished. If a colon or semi-colon is used instead of a full stop or dot, the writer wants to say more but is reluctant to pursue the matter.

Underlining

The paraph – the underline, underscore or flourish after a signature – was first introduced as a safeguard against forgery and therefore implies caution. In general, it retains that implication even today and in almost all cases it refers in some way to an underlying sense of caution.

Most graphologists suggest that a straightforward underlining of the signature implies a sense of confidence. Up to a point, this may be so, but that confidence is born of self-doubt, however slight, or however strong the writer may appear ordinarily. The heavier the pressure, the more energetic the writer and the most they will display enthusiasm in their dealings, but the position and style of the underlining implies limits to the amount of intimacy the writer will permit.

The underlining shown on the signature here indicates that the writer's sense of their own importance is being propped up and supported by the line drawn below. The signature arches first up, then down, implying enthusiasm. The paraph arches as well, another indication of a sensitive nature.

When the paraph is extended to encircle the name it is a sense of sheltering the self, withdrawal and anxiety.

A line over the signature, an overscore, shows the writer has a need for self-protection. There will be some selfishness in the make-up as well. If or when challenged, whether guilty or not, the writer will almost always exhibit a self-defensive attitude.

Should the writer use both an underscore and an overscore, the indication is one of loneliness and inner reserve. It is quite difficult for the writer to trust others; there is always that element of suspicion regarding their motives.

A double paraph under a signature is a sign of a selfish nature. Where this is the case, the writer is looking for recognition they feel is due, but whatever talent they have may not be as extensive as they think.

Elaborate curlicues always mean ostentation and an overactive ego. The degree of the design is usually only equalled by the writer's poor taste.

The half-paraph, a short line, placed under the first name only suggests the writer wants an informal relationship. When placed under the surname only, the writer wants matters kept on a formal basis – they may decide later if this can be changed.

If the first name has more than one syllable and there is a short paraph under the second part of that name, the writer is probably asking for their name not to be abbreviated.

If the paraph scores through the name or a part of the name, the writer will have difficulty in getting along with others. They are likely to be deceptive and have a rather shallow outlook. There will be a 'me-first' attitude at all times.

Signature slant

If the slant of the signature is different from that of the main body of the script, there is some divergence between the natural personality and the way the writer wishes to appear in public.

A left-slanted script followed by a right-slanted signature indicates an outwardly warm and affectionate nature, but only on the surface. This writer is basically unemotional and tends towards secrecy. They may seem to be demonstrative and easygoing but this external behaviour is cultivated and hides inner conflicts. Thus, the writer really is liable to have both a private and public image.

When a left-slanted signature follows a right-slanted script it is a sign of repression of the normal affectionate and sociable nature. Natural responses are suppressed, even controlled at times, perhaps due to emotional stress or domestic problems.

A signature written with a mixed slant indicates someone who is unstable and unreliable – certainly at the time of writing. This writer is inconsistent, unsettled and subject to the mood of the moment. They are also likely to display a lack of self-discipline.

In a signature where the lower zone strokes extend to the left, there may be some emotional and sexual repression and inhibition. This is probably largely due to an influence from the past that the writer has been unable, or is unwilling, to shake off. When the lower zone strokes tend to the right, the writer is outgoing, friendly and generally good natured.

Strokes that extend towards the left in the upper zone suggest the writer has high aspirations but these tend largely to remain just dreams. If the extensions are to the right in the upper zone, expect to find an actively ambitious type.

Capital letters

Over-emphasised capital letters in a signature betray poor taste and materialism. Status is everything, the writer will pursue a personal niche within the social framework of the group, society or environment in which they find themselves so they can take control. If the capitals are just slightly larger than average, the effect is not so marked but the writer will still display plenty of ambition to achieve positions of influence or responsibility. They may be collector – and not just of things but also people to control.

Capital letters the same size as the rest of the signature imply a fairly modest character, someone who does not stand out but who does make their mark in their own way.

Small capitals indicate a writer who undersells or undervalues their own worth. They display little ambition and, although they are likely to be quite good at their job, this writer just plods on from day to day.

Signatures of the famous

Signatures of famous – and infamous – people from both the past and the present are in great demand by collectors. This is especially so if the person died young and perhaps found fame after their death. Today there are a number of organisations dedicated to this collecting mania. Many books are available which show examples of the signatures of famous people.

An hour or two spent looking at the handwriting and signatures of figures from either the distant or recent past can be revealing. You will almost certainly find that there are other sides to their natures that others have failed to recognise or comment on. It is a great way to enjoy practising your skills.

John le Carré

Intelligent, well-written and with good taste, the thriller writer John le Carré has a signature expressing his keen intellect and ability to solve complex problems. The lack of pretentiousness is a sign of a well-bred mind and the rising slope reveals ambition. The arcade small n presupposes a writer who has a good sense of proportion and who knows instinctively what to reveal and what to keep to himself. He relies upon his instinct and intuition as well as reason.

The signature also shows creative qualities which, of course, he directs into his books.

Billy Connolly

The embellishments, whirls and loops circling over comedian Billy Connolly's signature indicate a proud, slightly egotistical personality with unusual tastes. The illegible surname shows materialistic urges and there is forcefulness in the long downstroke and angles. An exclamation mark at the end of his name indicates that he likes to have the last word.

Alec Guiness

Actor Alec Guiness gives very little away in his signature except the fact that he is a very private man with an intelligent and basically non-aggressive personality. The right slant shows his outward friendliness which is kept in check by his discriminate nature and sense of purpose. He gets down to things rapidly and doesn't like any form of ostentatiousness in his life. Fully aware of his own worth and capabilities, he has a modest, almost diffident disposition and yet the underlining tells of a strong sense of his own abilities.

Elton John

There is a difference between Elton John's first and last names as he has a rising slope to his signature which is made in two steps, a sign of versatility and individuality. The loops are a sign of sensitivity, although the angular strokes in 'Elton' reveal that his mind rules his emotions.

The loop on the bottom of 'John', turning to the left, indicates that he can be a fluent thinker and that he knows how to keep his own counsel when necessary. This is shown by the thread-like ending of the small n.

Margaret Thatcher

This has been written with great speed, indicating plenty of inner confidence and, together with the small angular style, suggests good overall control. Emotion is kept out of decision-making and the M of Margaret, ending below the base-line, implies a stubborn and quite inflexible nature.

The slight threading shows her quick mind and diplomatic skills. The over-exaggerated initial arch of the combined t-bar stroke and the letter h shows self-protection and defensiveness if anyone tries to tackle her.

This also indicates sympathy for anyone in trouble: she has been there herself and she understands, but when she shows this side of her nature she likes to keep public awareness of her acts to an absolute minimum.

The virtually straight paraph under the name emphasises a dominant and quite forceful ego.

HRH Prince Charles

This slightly reclined signature with the sharp pointed arch of the letter h shows strong sensitivity with a deeply inquisitive mind for what attracts at the time.

The signature is almost wholly written in an enlarged, middle-zone style, which reflects self-centredness and some conceit. When all the letters are connected like this, it shows he gets bored easily and may well have a power complex. If you stand up to him with the facts rather than an emotional appeal, he will listen. He can be a stern taskmaster.

The loops inside the letter a and the looped r suggests he is not always as honest with himself or others as he could be. He finds it hard to display his emotions openly.

The underlining with hooks at either end show a strong tenacity of purpose.

Diana, Princess of Wales

This large, middle-zone script with some disconnectedness shows a very impressionable character, easily swayed by any appeal to the emotional side of her character.

The writing is mainly upright with just a hint of a left slant with some angles in an otherwise arcade style, indicating a person who knew how to stand on her own two feet and would give as good as she got. The style shows she could be extremely independent – even rebellious at times – and could also have a very sharp tongue.

The whole suggests a façade, perhaps hiding a rather good actress. The width of the letters implies an extravagant nature that needs strong control, but someone who may give way under temptation.

The last letter ends in a downward stroke and is an indication of obstinacy.

Chapter 25

ASSESSMENT ALPHABET

We have spent some time looking at the many variations of writing with regard to its overall appearance, certain types of initial lead-in and ending strokes, capital letters, margins and so on.

Of equal importance is the way the individual lower case letters are formed. They all occupy the whole of the middle zone where we would normally assess a writer's self-control and confidence, their ego, emotional responsiveness, stability, general outlook and the level of honesty – or dishonesty – in their make-up. The way letters are individually formed is of great importance, especially so when characteristics are repeated on a regular basis, or when they only appear in a specific set of circumstances. When a certain letter is formed in a particular way just once, it should not be taken in isolation; look elsewhere for other, supportive evidence.

Some of the lower case letters are formed with ascenders, loops or strokes into the upper zone, or with descenders, loops and strokes into the lower zone. These have been dealt with in greater detail elsewhere in this book.

Make a list of all the features you observe and develop them gradually as you assess each aspect of the script and the individual letters within it. Carefully weigh up all the little facets of information; one may cancel out another or it may be supported by evidence from elsewhere in the script.

As this is an introductory guide, it is not possible to describe every variation you may encounter in the course of an analysis. However, it does offer a sound starting point for your considerations.

The letter a

It is quite usual for some letters to be left open on either side or at the top. Just occasionally, the bottom part of the letter may not be properly closed, especially in handwriting which is done quickly.

Variations in the way the letter a is formed are quite natural. If all the letters are narrow or cramped, the writer will have a closed mind, but if they are all broad, then the writer will be tolerant, imaginative and tend to be broad-minded.

Open at the top:
talkative

Open at the bottom:
dishonest

With a starting stroke:
cautious, unsure

Loop inside: not always
honest with themselves

Double loop inside:
deceptive with others

Narrow:
reserved, secretive

Wide:
broad-minded, tolerant

Square: possesses
manual dexterity

Angular base:
avaricious

Ending stroke below base-
line: stubborn, deliberate

Printed: possesses
creative inclinations

Definite ending stroke:
a dreamer, warm-natured

The letter b

This letter often appears together with another b and, when written in a clear and consistent way, it indicates good control and confidence. A clearly defined difference between the letters suggests the writer may have some inner emotional instability at the time of writing.

Open at the base:
deceptive, dishonest

No loop:
intelligent, perceptive

Like a figure 6: money
matters are important

Wide loop:
over-imaginative

Narrow loop:
shy, idealistic

Starting stroke:
fussy, unsure, slow

Open on the left:
critical, hypocritical

Angular base:
difficult, awkward

Cup too wide:
easily fooled, gullible

Pointed loop: quick
tempered, easily roused

The letter c

This letter usually has a starting stroke but when it does not, the writer will exhibit a high degree of self-confidence and even self-sufficiency. However slight any starting stroke may appear, it shows a certain amount of natural dependency or need for support from those around the writer. A large, wide letter implies open-mindedness, while a narrow, small letter indicates a shy or slightly reserved attitude.

Angular:
astute, clever, hot-tempered

Like a letter e:
self-centred

Starting stroke:
calculating, dependent

No starting stroke:
self-sufficient

Extended end:
self-admiring

Rounded:
warm-natured

Pointed top:
good perception

Pointed base:
likes their own way

Square appearance:
practical

The letter d

The letter d indicates sociability and some adaptability but wide variations in a script suggest sensitivity to criticism, no matter how well meant. When two letters d are together they should be identically formed to show consistency. Wide differences show a comparative emotional instability. The shorter the stem, the shorter the patience, especially if the stem appears broken.

Open at the base:
deceptive, hypocritical

Tent-like:
stubborn, taciturn

Small stem:
quiet, unassuming

Pot-lid:
difficult to get along with

Oval open at the top:
talkative, unreliable

Greek style:
cultured, perceptive

Wide loop: emotional,
sensitive, imaginative

Narrow loop:
emotionally repressed

Retraced or amended
downstroke: over-careful,
nervous

Knots in oval:
secretive, deceptive

Tall stem:
idealistic, a dreamer

The letter e

This letter often falls at the end of a word, sentence or line. The longer the ending stroke, the more defensive and cautious the writer. A short ending stroke indicates a brusque, no-nonsense type, one easily misunderstood. The larger the letter, the more talkative the writer, while the smaller it appears, the more the writer tends to play things close to their chest.

Narrow loop: secretive, shrewd

Angular: unsociable, temperamental

Greek form: refined, educated

Curled over final: self-protective, untruthful

Like a letter i: plain, straightforward

Vertical final: idealistic, a dreamer

Broad: talkative, style-conscious

Ending stroke under letter: selfish, thoughtless

Long ending stroke: generous, considerate

Final stroke with hooks: dislikes criticism, tenacious

Ending stroke below base: obstinate, inconsiderate

No ending stroke: cautious, careful

The letter f

A well-balanced letter f suggests inner contentment. This is the only trizonal letter so exaggeration of any of the zones will show a certain amount of imbalance in the nature. Large base loops always indicate plenty of physical energy, while over-large upper loops show an element of formality. Basically, this letter will help you to assess a writer's physical approach to their everyday life.

Balanced: well-organised, inwardly settled

Knotted middle: tenacious, tough

No lower loop: plenty of ideas, little follow-through

Reverse lower loop: independent with a rebel streak

No upper loop: energetic, self-reliant

Full upper loop: emotional, sensitive

Like a cross: fatalistic, quick-witted

Full lower loop: energetic, restless

Webbed base: deceitful, hypocritical

Unusual lower loops: possessing unusual sexual inclinations

Triangular base: poor sex life, selfish at home

The letter g

This letter indicates the strengths and weaknesses of the libido, physical energy and sexual nature. If the loops are all the same size they show controlled imagination. A variety of loops is one indication of poor physical co-ordination. The use of consistently different 'tails' to this letter reveals moodiness, but samples written at different times should be examined before you make a decision on this.

Large full loop: energetic with a strong sex drive

'X' loop: has a poor sex life or drive

Open loop: restless, loves change

Hooked ending stroke: acquisitive, avaricious

No loop: good judgement; determined if heavy

Low cross loop: poor sexual compatibility

Like a q: altruistic, with a poor sex drive

Ending stroke to left: likely to encounter sexual problems

Like a figure 8: financially resourceful, educated

Double loop: compulsive

The letter h

The upper stroke of the letter h should run parallel with the natural slant of the writing to show good control. If there is a variation, the writer will lack a consistent approach. A gap between the first downstroke and the upper stroke of the hoop indicates the writer is inwardly unsettled.

No loop: head rules the heart

Loop apart from stem: poor sense of responsibility

Large loop: sensitive, imaginative

Open loop: lack of responsibility

Small loop: original, humorous

Angular: aggressive, temperamental

Poor hoop: limited, unimaginative

Triangular loop: practical, can be awkward

Wide hoop: contented, confident

Long starting stroke: dependent, difficult to please

The letter i

When the base of the letter is the same or slightly larger than the middle zone, the writer moves and blends well in society. If the stem is smaller than the middle zone, the writer is insecure, introverted and lacks self-confidence.

When the lower case letter i is used as the personal pronoun it shows insecurity and immaturity. When seen continually through a script, this trait is emphasised.

Dot precisely over the stem: attentive to detail

Arc dot to the left: introverted, sharp-tongued

Dot to the left: cautious, tends to procrastinate

Circle dot: likes to impress, immature

Dot to the right: impulsive, natural

Wavy dot: humorous, fun-loving

Club or dash dot: earthy, impatient, temperamental

Connecting dot: intelligent, perceptive

Arc dot to the right: observant, creative

Variety of dots: imaginative, inconsistent, restless

The letter j

To assess dots, use the guidelines for the letter i. Heavy dots with a light stroke on the stem suggest inner uncertainty. These writers need plenty of encouragement. A large loop always indicates a wealth of physical energy. As a rule, this letter will help you to assess the writer's physical approach to everyday life.

Large full loop: energetic, enthusiastic

Angular: direct, temperamental

Arc or claw to the left: tends to avoid responsibility

Long, wide, open loop: impressionable, easily led

No loop: good judgement

Loop to the right: altruistic, perceptive

'X' loop: has poor sex life or drive

Curved downstroke: immature, dependent

Small loop: lacks energy and has poor drive

No dot: absent-minded, careless

The letter k

This letter indicates the amount of control needed for day-to-day matters. A consistent k shows control. Too much variety suggests a changeable or moody nature, although an analysis of the rest of the writing will confirm or soften this assessment. A k made with several strokes implies poor emotional control; a 'tied' or knotted k reveals much more care is used in personal relationships.

Long starting stroke: resentful, unsure

Tall upper loop: idealistic, formal

No upper loop: plain and simple, straightforward

Narrow upper loop: idealistic, sensitive to criticism

Large lower loop: awkward, rebellious, defiant

Knotted stem: careful, inhibited

Printed: open, creative

Long arms: affectionate, demonstrative

Short arms: shy or reticent, undemonstrative

Separate strokes: untrustworthy, not genuine

The letter l

Depending on how it is constructed, this letter shows emotional strengths and weaknesses. When two are placed together, they should be uniformly made for this indicates inner emotional balance. If they are uneven, the writer will be subject to moods and unable to control their emotional feelings and responses. If all the letters l are uniformly written throughout the script, then the writer exerts too much personal control.

Tall wide loop: sensitive, emotional, idealistic

No loop: self-confident, has a quick mind

Angular: brusque, selfish

Covering stroke: narrow-minded, cautious

Small loop: shy, timid

Long ending stroke: kind, generous

Ending stroke below baseline: mean, blunt

Pointed loop: selfish, temper easily roused

The letter m

A wide letter m suggests carelessness and extravagance. If it is narrow, the writer lacks confidence. When the first hoop is low, they are largely dependent on the opinions of those around. If the second loop is low, they are more outgoing. A balanced letter m suggests a well-balanced inner nature.

No middle stroke: freedom-loving, avoids responsibility

Three loops: hides real feelings, superficial

First hoop high: proud, selfish

Like a u: health and diet-conscious

Second hoop high: insecure, dependent on others

Three hoops: insecure, compulsive

Well-balanced: sharing, compatible

Ending stroke below baseline: abrupt, selfish

Angular: lacks humour, ambitious

Short ending stroke: loner, avoids involvement

Central loop: has a controlling nature

The letter n

This letter's shape may frequently alter in a sample. If the variation is marked, it suggests that the writer is a poor planner. Sometimes, the letter may be written larger than the rest of the script. This can be due to lowered intelligence, immaturity or childishness or, with other signs to support this assessment, just plain tiredness.

Narrow: inhibited, shy or insecure

Like a u: soft, warm and friendly

Wide: open, frank, confident

Wavy line: changeable, yielding

Angular: to the point, analytical

With loops: a worrier, insecure

Tapering: has a sense of humour, diplomatic

Square: dextrous, practical

Like a v: hard, analytical

The letter o

The letter o should always appear as perfectly formed as possible, as this reflects a basically honest nature, someone who is warm, generous and nice to know. Anything wider than this means an overreaching of natural reserves. A narrow letter o indicates implies inner worry, self-doubt and a rather introverted character.

Two letters o together should be uniformly constructed, for that shows self-control. When there are decided differences, the writer will to be selfish.

Wide: broad-minded, easy to get along with

Narrow: inhibited, secretive

Top open: untrustworthy, talkative

Base open: dishonest, hypocritical

Knotted at the top: cold, distant

Inner line(s); deceitful with self or others, unreliable

Heart-shaped: a born romantic, emotional

Double circle: self-protective, difficult to get to know

Straight line through: perceptive, shrewd

The letter p

The letter p helps to determine a writer's physical inclinations, interest in sport or other outdoor pursuits and interests. If two are written together they should be of a uniform appearance. This indicates the level of physical co-ordination the writer will display. When they are decidedly different, the writer is likely to be unpredictable and show a poor level of common sense. There will also be poor physical control.

Loop on top of stem: sensitive, emotional, yielding

Angular lead-in: hard, contentious, emotional

Separate strokes: dextrous, creative

Long base loop: energetic, full of stamina, outdoor type

Large loop: nosy, many fingers in many pies

Small loop: narrow-minded, pessimistic

Open at baseline: hard, dishonest, cruel

Pot-lid: wilful, determined

Downstroke to the left: cannot let go of the past

Retraced loop: full of staying power, fit

The letter q

This is a difficult letter to write fluently so the better it is written, the more control is exerted by the writer. Any small strokes in the middle zone oval suggest secrecy or deception. When it looks like a number 9 there may be a musical or mathematical inclination.

Claw to the left:
dislike of responsibility

Claw to the right:
egotistical, selfish

Long upward final:
warm nature, obliging

Straight downstroke:
energetic, direct

Triangular loop:
difficult to get along with

Open on base line:
unreliable

Open to the left:
talkative, critical

Separate strokes:
dextrous, creative

The letter r

Because the letter r can occur at the beginning, middle or end of a word, there can be up to as many as six or seven different styles in one sample, which is fairly acceptable. However, the starting letters r should all be the same, as should all those in the middle or at the end of a word. If they all look the same, the writer exerts strong control over their responses.

A small letter r indicates shows pessimism and small-mindedness. The larger it is, the more optimistic and broad-minded the writer will be. Occasionally, a printed capital will appear instead of the normal lower case. This suggests a bad temper that can flare up very quickly.

Like a v: poor social
adaptability, inquisitive

Like a u:
open, friendly

Flat top:
broad-minded, constructive

One peak:
streak of curiosity, critical

Two peaks: versatile,
good with their hands

Plain and simple: good
perception, enthusiastic

Small:
narrow-minded, carping

Large:
broad-minded, sociable

Greek form:
artistic, creative

The letter s

The letter s can start a word, be in the middle or at the end so there can be several different types in one sample, which is reasonably acceptable. However, all the starting letters should be the same, as should all those in the middle or at the end of a word. If they all look the same, the writer has good control over their emotions. The small letter s indicates emotional sensitivity; the larger it is, the less the writer is concerned with other people's feelings.

Pointed top: acid-tongued, critical

Round: kindly natured, easily swayed

Large: idealistic, imaginative

Small: reserved, shy

Long lead-in: determined, persistent

Dollar sign: concerned with money, acquisitive

Open at baseline: easily led, gullible

Angular: aggressive, determined, selfish

Like a pawn: callous, with a hard streak

Ampersand: unfeeling, moody

Underclaw: avaricious, selfish

The letter t

The letter t can be written in countless different ways and have such a wide variation in the cross-bars that it is rare to see a consistently formed letter every time. The t indicates the amount of emotion, intelligence, perception, personal discipline, self-control and will-power. Expect to find variety when you look for this letter in any one sample. This letter is often used to determine the speed of handwriting.

Tent-like stem: stubborn, pushy

Tall stem: idealistic, aspirational

Small stem: lacks confidence, retiring

Spread stem: slow, lazy

Loop in stem: sensitive, imaginative

Cross bar omitted: careless, thoughtless

Bar at top: ambitious, desires to lead

Low bar: lack of ambition, easy-going

Bar to the left: hesitant, slow

Bar to the right: impulsive, perceptive

Ascending bar:
controlling, ambitious

Like a figure 7: dislikes
opposition, hard-natured

Descending bar:
critical, difficult

Like a cross:
fatalistic, superstitious

Hooks on bar:
temperamental, unsociable

The letter u

Basically, this letter indicates emotional adaptability and the type of social nature to which the writer may aspire. It is often written slightly larger than the rest of the script and this can suggests a certain amount of self-doubt. In certain circumstances, the writer may be uncertain of how they should react rather than just acting naturally. Thus, with this letter, what you see may not always be what you get!

Square:
practical, constructive

Small:
socially minded, a follower

Wavy:
versatile, diplomatic

Deep:
imaginative, intense

Wide:
broad-minded, acquisitive

Shallow:
quiet, unassuming

Like a v:
difficult, awkward

The letter v

Basically, this an angular letter but is often softened to seem more rounded and it can appear slightly larger than the rest of the script. This is a measure of how well a writer can contain their emotional energies. Some authorities suggest that the sexual response of the writer can be determined from the way the letter is formed.

Like a u:
easygoing, friendly

Wide: broad-minded,
sexy, a spendthrift

First stroke longer:
selfish, determined

Like an x:
unreliable, untrustworthy

Second stroke longer:
enterprising, takes chances

Incurved ending stroke:
defensive, self-protective

Narrow:
shy, reserved, critical

Unconnected:
promises much, delivers little

The letter w

This letter tells of the ambitions of the writer. Rounded bases always suggest a defensive or self-protective, yielding nature but the writer tends to move easily in society no matter what their inner feelings may be. The angular form shows drive and enthusiasm, frequently misplaced and often without thinking things through properly first.

Incurved ending stroke: defensive, self-protective

Wide: broad-minded, socially active

Narrow: inhibited, shy

Angular: shrewd, perceptive, suffers from inner tensions

Rounded: sensitive, gentle, easygoing

Looped middle: clever, conceited

Looped ending stroke: immature, faddy

Three loops: smooth, vain, uses people

Three arches: secretive, opportunistic

Tall lead-in: over-confident, untrustworthy

The letter x

This letter shows how well the writer gets along with others in either in a close relationship or as a casual friend. A badly formed letter x in an otherwise good script may be as a result of frustration; perhaps because the writer was unable to cope with a situation at the time.

Joined curves: shy, careful socially

Looped cross: has a good mind, perceptive

Separate strokes: has difficulty relating, a loner

Ending stroke below baseline: aggressive, opinionated

Straight lines: hard, unyielding

The letter y

The letter y reflects the sexual inclinations of the writer. If all the lower loops are made in exactly the same way, the sexual nature is probably repressed, held back in some way, through a lack of imagination or because of a recent relationship break-up. Variations in the lower loop suggest an easily stimulated and responsive emotional and sexual life.

Open loop: changeable, restless

Arch to the left: clannish, dislikes responsibility

Double loop: compulsive

Frogfoot loop: sexually incompatible

Unusual loop: has unusual sexual interests

Long downstroke: sexually restless, outdoor type

Small loop: has little interest in physical sex

Short downstroke: repressed sexual nature

Large loop: has a healthy libido, materialistic, driven

'X' loop: has a poor sex life or drive

Triangular base: has a poor sex life, selfish at home

The letter z

It is quite rare to see this letter repeated in the same way in any one sample. It is not easy to keep the writing flowing so any unusual variations probably relate to writer's mood at the time.

Rounded: easygoing, gentle

Central loop: awkward, stubborn

Angular: unyielding, opinionated

Long ending stroke: vain, egotistical

Like a figure 3: materialistic, careful

Unusual shape: sexy, has a vivid imagination

Printed: straightforward, confident

ASSESSMENT NOTES

The pages of this chapter can be copied for personal use only so that you can create your own graphology assessments. You will not need to fill in every section each time, but the headings should act as a reminder as to the elements you should be thinking about at each stage. Jot down brief notes as you go through so that you can then create an overall assessment at the end, which takes all the pieces of evidence into account.

Name: . . . .

Age: . . . . **Sex:** . . . .

Nationality: . . . .

. . . .

Schooling: . . . .

. . . .

Other information: . . . .

. . . .

. . . .

Right-handed/left-handed: . . . .

1 **Form level**   *Level of intelligence and maturity*

Topic	Descriptive comments	Conclusions
Form level		
Speed		
Pressure		
General spacing		

2 **Rhythm**   *Mental, physical and spiritual forces*

Topic	Descriptive comments	Conclusions
Connecting strokes		
Spacing		
Letter formation		
Size		

3 Release and restraint   *Emotional life*

Topic	Descriptive comments	Conclusions
Control level		

4 Margins   *Social skills*

Topic	Descriptive comments	Conclusions
Description of margins		

5 Spacing   *Clarity of thought; relating to other people*

Topic	Descriptive comments	Conclusions
Spacing around letters		
Spacing between letters		
Width of letters		
Speed		
Pressure		

6 Connections   *Fundamental personality*

Topic	Descriptive comments	Conclusions
Arcade		
Angular		
Garland		
Thread		

7 Zones   *Levels of realism and idealism; personal maturity*

Topic	Descriptive comments	Conclusions
Upper zone		
Middle zone		
Lower zone		

8 Legibility   *Sincerity and consideration*

Topic	Descriptive comments	Conclusions
Legible		
Illegible		

9 Pressure   *Mood and vitality*

Topic	Descriptive comments	Conclusions
Heavy pressure		
Moderate pressure		
Light pressure		
Speed		

10 **Starting and ending strokes** *Speed of thought and caution*

Topic	Descriptive comments	Conclusions
Starting strokes		
Ending strokes		

11 **Size** *Value placed on emotion*

Topic	Descriptive comments	Conclusions
Large		
Medium		
Small		

12 Slant   *Forward- or backward-looking*

Topic	Descriptive comments	Conclusions
Forward slant		
Backward slant		
Vertical writing		
Mixed slant		

13 Capital letters   *Self-regard and self-expression*

Topic	Descriptive comments	Conclusions
Large capitals		
Small capitals		
Capital I		

14 i-dots   *Personality development*

Topic	Descriptive comments	Conclusions
Position of dot		
Pressure of dot		
Shape of dot		

15 **Lower case t**   *Personality development*

Topic	Descriptive comments	Conclusions
Position of bar		
Shape of bar		
Slope of bar		
Consistency of style		

16 Numbers   *Concern with material matters*

Topic	Descriptive comments	Conclusions
Position		
Base-line		
Slant		
Form		
Pressure		
Columns		
Alterations		

17 Punctuation   *Precision and mood*

Topic	Descriptive comments	Conclusions
Style		
Accuracy		
Consistency		
Placement		

18 Envelopes *Public image*

Topic	Descriptive comments	Conclusions
Legibility		
Comparison with writing inside		
Size		
Placement of address		
Encircled capitals		
Underlining		
Unusually shaped letters		
Slant		

19 Ink and paper colour   *Personality and mood*

Topic	Descriptive comments	Conclusions
Ink colour		
Paper colour		

20 Loops   *Emotion, sensuality and sex drive*

Topic	Descriptive comments	Conclusions
Pressure		
Slant		
Size of loops		
Shape of loops		

21 Vocational guidance   *Career direction and compatibility*

Topic	Descriptive comments	Conclusions
Handwriting slant		

22 Doodles   *Preoccupations*

Topic	Descriptive comments	Conclusions
Rounded		
Angular		
Representational		
Letters or words		
Figures		
Position		
Ink colour		

23 Signatures *Projected self-image*

Topic	Descriptive comments	Conclusions
Position		
Size		
General attributes		
Underlining		
Slant		
Capital letters		

24 Alphabet   *Confidence, honesty, emotional stability*

Topic	Descriptive comments	Conclusions
a		
b		
c		
d		
e		
f		
g		
h		
i		

Topic	Descriptive comments	Conclusions
j		
k		
l		
m		
n		
o		
p		
q		
r		

Topic	Descriptive comments	Conclusions
s		
t		
u		
v		
w		
x		
y		
z		

25 Additional comments

26 Final personality assessment

INDEX